THE PORTABLE STANFORD

PUBLISHED BY THE
STANFORD ALUMNI ASSOCIATION

MIDLIFE
IN
PERSPECTIVE

BY
HERANT
KATCHADOURIAN

STANFORD ALUMNI ASSOCIATION
STANFORD, CALIFORNIA

THE PORTABLE STANFORD is a series publication of the Stanford Alumni Association. Each book is an original work written expressly for this series by a member of the Stanford University faculty. The PS series is designed to bring the widest possible sampling of Stanford's intellectual resources into the homes of alumni. It includes books based on current research as well as books that deal with philosophical issues, which by their nature reflect to a greater degree the personal views of their authors.

THE PORTABLE STANFORD
Stanford Alumni Association
Bowman Alumni House
Stanford, California 94305

Library of Congress Catalog Card
Number 86-63344
ISBN: 0-916318-22-2

To the memory of
my mother, Efronia,
a master in the art of life

CONTENTS

ACKNOWLEDGMENTS

Even a short book requires a lot of help. I was ably assisted in this effort by the editorial expertise of Miriam Miller and Carol King, while Gayle Hemenway tirelessly kept the production of the book on the move and Laurie Burmeister typed and retyped the successive drafts of the manuscript.

Many friends and colleagues offered advice and encouragement, as exemplified by Martin and Mariella Evans, and my wife, Stina.

Special thanks are due Bob Ciano for designing the book and to Nigel Holmes for creating the charts. Their great talents have much enriched this work.

FOREWORD AND FOREWARNING

Introductions would serve a useful function if they clearly and forthrightly told the reader what to expect. The reader is thereby forewarned and either drops the book or gets into it with reasonable expectations.

These considerations are particularly apt when one is dealing with a subject so broad and encompassing—as is the case here—that one could encounter a wide variety of treatments of the subject.

This book attempts to describe for you the salient physiological and psychological changes that characterize the passage through midlife. It is meant to help you understand what happens to your body, sexuality, mind, personality, intimate relationships, and career in midlife. Since there are many volumes on any one of these topics, my treatment is, by necessity, highly selective. In each case, I provide enough detail to give substance and specificity to the discussion without trying to be comprehensive.

The focus of this book is on information, not advice; its perspective is instructive, not prescriptive. Even if you wanted my advice, what kind of advice could I give you, not knowing who you are? Nonetheless, this book is not meant to be solely an intellectual exercise and I do hope that what I have to say will be of some use to you.

If you are searching for diets, exercise regimens, aphrodisiacs, or ways of improving your memory, saving your marriage, finding a spouse, or salvaging your career, you may do better to look elsewhere. And if you find a book that embodies the secrets of how to deal effectively with these problems, all in a couple of hundred pages, please let me know about it. I want to read it too.

What I offer you here are the pertinent facts, so far as I have been able to ascertain them, about the most important aspects of midlife so that you may explore further those that interest you. More importantly, I hope that what you read in these pages will make you reflect and find your own truths about yourself. The suggestions for further readings included in the endnotes may also prove helpful.

The tone of this book is neither upbeat nor downbeat but *on*beat. There is much in what I say that should give you comfort and satisfaction. But there are also things that you will perhaps not like to hear. In that case, please remember that I am but the messenger who is telling you what is out there in the world—as is it is now, not as it ought to be.

My perspective is that of a teacher rather than a researcher or advocate. I believe we should approach each phase of life with realism and compassion. Otherwise our perspective becomes too fixed or too vague. Being fifty, or middle-aged, is no better or worse than being any other age. Every season has its own joys and sorrows. As Sir Thomas Browne put it three hundred years ago:

> Confound not the distinctions of thy life which nature hath divided; that is, youth, adolescence, manhood, and old age: nor in these divided periods, wherein thou art in a manner four, conceive thyself but one. Let every division be happy in its proper virtues, nor one vice run through all. Let each distinction have its salutary transition, and critically deliver thee from the imperfections of the former; so ordering the whole, that prudence and virtue may have the largest section.

1

THE
RHYTHM
OF
LIFE

Turning fifty. The "Big Five-O." Wonderful like the dawn of a new age, brimming with promise of fulfillment? Or ominous like a tanker coming at you through the fog? Which is it? What happens at age fifty?

I approached my fiftieth birthday with great expectations. There were no major crises in my professional or personal life. But there were many loose ends on all fronts, and I firmly believed that as I turned fifty, these loose ends would get tied up; I would get closure on issues that for years had drained and distracted me like so many dripping faucets.

My expectations of turning fifty were entangled with my sense of being fully adult. Mind you, this had nothing to do with external evidence of being adult. I acted mature enough as an adolescent to pass for an adult when I turned twenty. The issue did not involve objective accomplishments or the perception of others but had to do with my own perception of what it meant to be adult. And to me that meant doing what I thought I ought to do with my life.

The day finally came when I turned fifty. For a short while there was the illusion that the long-awaited closure had been attained. But then I could hear the faucets dripping again, and I realized with some amusement that no magical transformation had taken place. I continued to change ever so slightly—sometimes for the better, sometimes for the worse—but most of the time into someone merely a little different.

My experience of turning fifty is neither typical nor atypical. It has some features common to the experience of others and some features that are more idiosyncratic.

THE MANY WAYS OF FACING FIFTY

For a broader perspective on the range of experience of both men and women in this phase of life, let us consider some biographical vignettes based on actual cases (names and certain details have been changed). These examples do not represent a statistically random sample of fifty-year-olds. Rather they have been selected to portray some of the more common life circumstances of those around the age of fifty as well as a few examples of more unusual patterns. There may be nothing particularly novel or startling in any of these stories for you. As a matter of fact, after a few moments of reflection you could probably come up with an equivalent set of tales yourself. The point of the exercise is to get a sense of the real-life contexts in which fifty-year-olds are likely to find themselves.

Robert Wilson is a hospital administrator and his wife, Carol, a schoolteacher. Their youngest child has just left for college. They have both been quite successful in their chosen careers but have gone as far as they are likely to. Their working lives are going to remain more or less the same, but they like what they do. They do not feel "stuck" and they have no intention of changing careers or jobs. They have had a solid marriage but not very much time for each other because of the demands of their work and their children. They now look forward to a period of greater intimacy and to more opportunities for doing things together, as well as to pursuing their own independent interests.

Jane Brown, forty-eight, married but not for much longer, has three children, the youngest of whom is seventeen. Her husband has announced his intention of leaving. She had always thought they had a moderately successful marriage albeit not a particularly exciting relationship. Not only does she now face losing a mate, but soon after that her last child will leave for college. The one thing she can hold on to is her house; in anticipation of the separation, however, her husband has refinanced it, so in five years she may well lose the house too. Jane had a family inheritance but it was melded into community property. Although she is college educated, she has acquired little work experience to put on a job application. She wants to go back to work or possibly to night school for specialized training but is not yet certain how to go about it. Her children are supportive of her and she feels optimistic but anxious about the future.

Henry Brown, forty-nine, estranged husband of Jane Brown, is vice-president of a company but not likely to get much further. Although he has done reasonably well, he has fallen far short of his ambitions. He feels that he has hit a dead end in his career yet sees little likelihood of being able to do much about it. He has, however, met a young woman during a business trip, and their affair has worked wonders for his sagging sense of self-esteem. Unlike his professional life, his personal life is subject to his control so he has decided to leave his wife and children. His feelings of excitement about the future are marred by his sense of guilt. He is fond of his children and has invested a great deal in them, but they have now turned against him for abandoning their mother.

Frank Cooper, forty-eight, had been a plumber all his working life, and as a master plumber he earned good wages. But suddenly the company for which he had worked for fifteen years fired all of its union employees and replaced them with nonunion workers at much lower wages. Frank and two of his friends formed their own plumbing company, which did so well that by the time he was fifty-three, Frank's work was largely managerial, and he was earning more money than ever before. He and his wife look forward to many more good years of living comfortably together and enjoying their children and grandchildren.

Teresa Bertolli's husband died of a heart attack when she was forty-five and had just gone back to work. Although two of their three children were still in college, her husband's estate made it possible for her to continue living in her own house and paying for her children's education. Her work, which had been a part-time avocation, became a full-time career. By the time she reached fifty, she was well established professionally and had a wide circle of friends. Her children keep in close touch with her.

Peter Burke, fifty, teaches physics at a small college. His wife, Pauline, forty-seven, is a nurse turned computer programmer. The Burkes have no children, but they have been supporting Peter's parents over the last ten years. His parents are both quite elderly, housebound, and intermittently ill. The Burkes have not had an extended vacation for years and find it difficult to plan for the future as long as his parents are still alive.

Sara Stein went from college to the elite training squad of a major department store. She rose rapidly to become an important buyer, traveling extensively and handling large sums of money. Her work was stimulating and exciting for a while, but as the years went by she wanted to do something more intellectually demanding and satisfying. She went back to school part-time, eventually enrolled as a full-time graduate student, and obtained her Ph.D. in English at age fifty. She taught for two years, then decided she would rather be an editor; she began as a freelancer and within three years was appointed editor of a medical journal. She has never married.

Roger Letterman, forty-eight, had a brilliant career as an engineer and then moved into management. Rising rapidly through the ranks, he was appointed vice-president of his company and is virtually certain to become chief executive officer within the next few years. His wife, Priscilla, has a master's degree in art history but has never worked outside the home. With both of their children launched on successful careers, she is heavily immersed in their social life, serves on the board of the art museum in their city, and is active in a number of voluntary organizations. The future appears full of promise for both of them.

These examples could be multiplied endlessly if we were to look at the lives of people from broader socioeconomic, ethnic, geographic, and cultural backgrounds, and from different countries and cultures. As we expanded this circle, it would become increasingly difficult to answer the question, "What does it mean to turn fifty?" But in middle-class American society at least, almost everyone seems to be aware of crossing a line at age fifty, although the significance and the manifestations of that crossing vary widely.

What we have is a characteristic set of events and a date. The two may or may not coincide, although they are typically not far apart. Certain physiological and psychological changes occur during the two decades of middle age, stretching from about age forty to age sixty. Somewhere in the middle of this period we pass a significant landmark that we associate with age fifty. These changes will occur whether or not you are aware of the march of time. Yet awareness of the "50" sign on your life's calendar will focus your attention on what is happening, organize your experience, and influence your behavior to conform to commonly held norms.

FIFTY AS A METAPHOR

Turning fifty has become a metaphor in our culture for marking the peak of midlife, the middle of middle age.[1] Reaching fifty represents turning a corner—not like a car swerving sharply around a bend, but more like a ship gently plowing an arc in the sea.

Since life changes are gradual, our awareness of their shifts tends to be saltatory, coming in leaps and bounds. One morning you glance at your face or view your body in the mirror and are jolted into awareness that you have physically changed since you last looked closely at yourself. A popular tune or a public face from the past will nudge your recognition of what generation you belong to. Running into a friend you have not seen for a while, you might say, "You haven't changed at all," as you scrutinize the many, many changes that your friend has undergone. There are also important generational *markers* that indicate you have now entered a new phase of life: the last child leaving home for college, for example, or the birth of the first grandchild.

The focus of this book must be understood in terms of the metaphorical significance of age fifty. Age fifty makes sense only in the context of middle age, and the concept of middle age itself is meaningful only when placed in the broader context of the entire life span.

Time and Aging: Time is a human construct, but the process of aging has a basic uniformity at its biological bedrock. Not only do we physically age more or less the way people have always aged, but the underlying processes of aging have much in common with comparable events among animals.

It is not possible to age without the passage of time, and time cannot pass without our aging. Yet the rate at which aging occurs among people is not fixed. Some people age faster than others and most people have aged faster during some periods than during others. The pace of growing older is now slower than at any other time in history. Hence to be fifty years old at present is different, in purely physiological terms, from being fifty even in the earlier decades of this century. People are living longer, remaining healthier, and behaving differently. If you look at the photographs of your parents and grandparents when they were your current age—especially if you are in your middle or later years—and compare their looks with yours, this shift will be quite apparent.

Time in History: Time (Old English, "interval between events") represents an irreversible continuum. No matter what happens, time marches on relentlessly with no possibility of breaking stride or going back.

The ancient Greeks conceived of time as the divine river Oceanos which encircled the earth. Depicted as a mythical snake (*ouroboros*) perpetually swallowing its own tail, it symbolized eternity.[2] The Greeks also called time *chronos*, and identified it with the god Kronos (Saturn for the Romans), the father of Zeus. The image of Saturn as an old man armed with a scythe, devouring everything, including his own children, was transformed in the Christian era into the more benign figure of Father Time, at whose bidding Death snuffed out a person's life at the appointed hour.

Clocks and calendars that rule modern lives are the most palpable monitors of the passage of time. But there are also natural phenomena to remind us of its flux. The alternation of day and night, the passage of seasons, the cycles of birth and death—all these keep us aware of our own temporal journey. But the calculus of time must not be allowed to rule our lives. "To divide one's life by years," says Clifton Fadiman, "is of course to tumble into a trap set by our own arithmetic. The calendar consents to carry on its dull wall-existence by the arbitrary timetables we have drawn up in consultation with those permanent commuters, Earth and Sun. But we, unlike trees, need grow no annual rings."[3]

The passage of time is inextricably tied to the realities of life and death. The Greeks expressed this by their belief in a vital life-fluid (*aion*), which determined a person's allotted life span. When death liberated the soul from the body, it appeared near the grave of the deceased in the form of a snake (a belief shared by the Egyptians).

THE SPAN
OF LIFE

The notion of a fixed time allotment for life is still very much with us. Biologists conceive of it as the genetically determined maximum life span of a species. It is estimated at 175 years for a Galapagos tortoise, 110 years for a human, 30 years for a chicken, 3 years for a mouse. Accounts of people who are said to have lived longer have not been adequately substantiated.

How this genetic clock operates no one really knows. Cells have a limited life span. In laboratory tissue cultures, fibroblasts from the lungs of embryos will divide about fifty times and no more (the "Hayflick limit"). Although these experiments do not replicate actual living conditions in the body, they strongly suggest that the time during which cells can perpetuate themselves is limited. Since cells are the living units of the body, this limitation offers a plausible explanation for the finite life span of the organism as a whole.

There is no evidence that the maximum length of the human *life span* has changed during the last 100,000 years. What has changed is the average *life expectancy*, which has been steadily increasing (see Figure 1-1). Life expectancy has risen from a very rough estimate of eighteen years in Early Bronze Age Greece (the period of the Mycenaean civilization) to nearly age seventy-five currently in the United States, and is expected to reach age eighty by the year 2000.

These average figures are computed on the basis of how many people within a population die at each age. In earlier times, a substantial segment of the population died in infancy and childhood; in the United States and other industrialized countries this is no longer

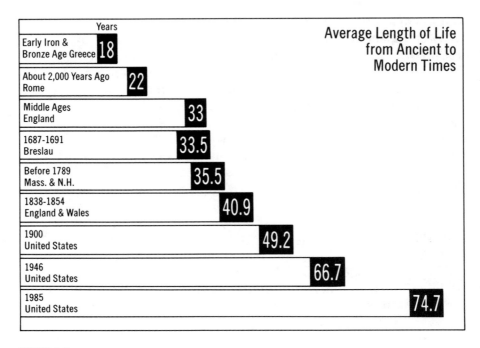

	Years
Early Iron & Bronze Age Greece	18
About 2,000 Years Ago Rome	22
Middle Ages England	33
1687-1691 Breslau	33.5
Before 1789 Mass. & N.H.	35.5
1838-1854 England & Wales	40.9
1900 United States	49.2
1946 United States	66.7
1985 United States	74.7

Average Length of Life from Ancient to Modern Times

FIGURE 1-1.

the case. The reduction in infant mortality is thus largely, though not entirely, responsible for the gains in life expectancy; today there are also many more people who live longer.

Since 1840, the survival curves have been pushed upward but their end point has not changed, as shown in Figure 1-2. Note that in 1840 only about half the population survived to age fifty. With each successive period the proportion of premature deaths decreases, so that in 1980, 50 percent of the population is surviving until almost eighty. As survival curves become flattened at the top (or "rectangularized"), they approximate more closely the ideal curve which we would have were there no premature deaths.

Based on actuarial statistics, we can tell at any given age how much time we have left on the average. At present, a fifty-year-old American woman can expect to live another twenty-nine years, to age seventy-nine; a fifty-year-old man, twenty-three more years, to age seventy-three. Some will beat these odds and others will go before their time. But these are the lines of credit on time that most of those who have made it to fifty can expect.

THE PERCEPTION
OF TIME

Time as an abstract concept is an objective and invariant entity; an hour is an hour anytime, anywhere on earth. Yet our perception of time is quite subjective. When you are stranded at an airport or otherwise watching the clock anxiously, time seems to pass very slowly. At other times, it seems to hurry away. ("Where did the summer go?")

The sense that time is running out is a common preoccupation during these years. It is as if you were using up a limited amount of money in a savings account that has accrued no interest and to which no new funds can be added. Assuming you will live to age eighty, age ten represents 12.5 percent and age fifty, 62.5 percent of your "capital" in the bank of time. The sense of time urgency will be even more acute if you feel that not only is there less and less time left, but what is left of it is passing away faster. Pound captures this feeling in a poem:

> The leaves fall early this autumn, in wind.
> The paired butterflies are already yellow with August
> Over the grass in the West garden;
> They hurt me. I grow older.[4]

The analogy to a savings account is, of course, imperfect. None of us, at any age, has a guaranteed credit line on the future. The only time that is ours is the time we have already spent. Nonetheless, it is quite sensible to assume that the law of averages will apply, give or take a few years, in most instances. And in the light of that, the fact that a fifty-year-old has quite a few years ahead is a source of both comfort and concern.

It has occurred to me that were I to live as long as my mother, I would have forty years ahead of me. That is as long as I have lived since the age of twelve—essentially my whole life beyond childhood. Yet the next forty years could not be merely a variant of the last forty years of my life. As Carl Jung has said, "We cannot live the afternoon of life according to the programme of life's morning; for what was great in the morning will be little at evening, and what in the morning was true will at evening have become a lie."[5]

For a professional man or woman the first half of adult life is like an obstacle course: College, perhaps graduate school, getting established in a career, and rising steadily within the ranks is the expected

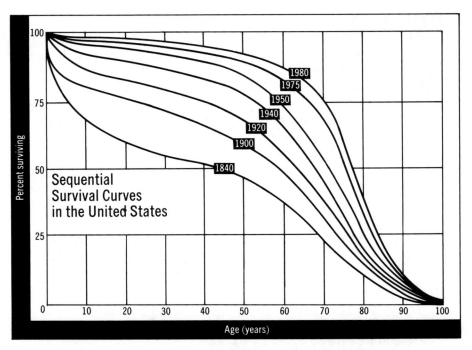

FIGURE 1-2. The progressive elimination of premature death allows these curves to begin to approximate the curve that would be found in the absence of any premature death.

norm. At midlife, this progression stops for most people. They have reached a plateau and the years stretch ahead to an uneventful future. The prospect of no further advancement to someone who has counted on it as a measure of success is quite distressing, and those who have been standing still all along have even more to worry about.

There are a few whose careers catapult in midlife (Margaret Thatcher became Prime Minister of England at fifty-three) and others who throw in the towel altogether. But these are the exceptions. The dilemma facing most of us at midlife is that there is too little time to do much and too much time to do little. Ivan Turgenev perceived it as "that vague, crepuscular time, the time of regrets that resemble hopes, of hopes that resemble regrets, when youth has passed, but old age has not yet arrived."[6]

A common shift in time orientation in the middle years is based on the realization that the time left to live is steadily losing out to the time one has lived: Whereas in the first half of life one tends to count the years already lived, in the second half one turns to the future and focuses on the years left to live.[7]

This shift in temporal perspective is but one of the consequences of the heightened awareness of one's mortality. At the turn of the century, when the average life expectancy in the United States was forty-nine years, any time beyond fifty was a bonus. That is no longer the case, yet the prospect of death cannot fail to become more palpable as our parents begin to die and some of our contemporaries suffer heart attacks or develop cancer. The issue of one's mortality, hitherto recognized in an abstract sense, now becomes more of a personal reality, albeit a reality still lodged in the indefinite future. We have always known that people die; now we each must face the fact that one day "I myself am going to die."

VARIETIES OF TIME

With respect to the events of the life cycle, the concept of time needs to be viewed in three dimensions: chronological time, social time, and historical time. We have so far focused mainly on the first dimension, *chronological age*. This measure is indispensable yet crude at best.

Chronological age is most useful in describing the developmental level of children. Childhood is a period of rapid change into which many developmental events are compressed in a fairly predictable manner. The differences, for example, between a three-year-old child and a four-year-old—or a two-year-old—are quite dramatic. Yet as those children enter adolescence, chronological age becomes a less reliable measure of development because of the wide variability in the onset and progress of puberty. One thirteen-year-old girl may still be a prepubescent child, another biologically mature enough to bear children.

The significance of chronological age becomes further confounded in adulthood. Except for the menopause, there are no biological markers at this time comparable to the changes of puberty. Social correlates of chronological age are so variable that they fail to tell us with any specificity where an individual stands on the scale of adult development. Appearance varies greatly. Some fifty-year-olds seem much younger and others much older than their actual age. Blind reliance on chronological age can be highly misleading. That a person is fifty, in the sense of having lived fifty years, does not tell all there is to know about that person.

Yet we are so highly susceptible to the presumed significance of age, especially when we cross landmark birthdays like fifty, that there is a tendency to subordinate our own perception of how we look and feel to the presumed norms of how we *should* look and feel at a given age. People often say, "But she doesn't look fifty" or "He doesn't act like fifty" or "I don't feel fifty," as if there were some prescribed or divinely ordained way of looking, acting, or feeling fifty.

The second chronological dimension is that of *social time*. Societies are typically age-graded. Age norms determine the culturally defined appropriate time for taking on various roles and living up to predetermined cultural expectations. Some of these transitions, such as puberty, are biologically based and often marked in various cultures by rites of passage. Even though our society has few clearly defined rituals to mark such passages, age norms still operate to impose certain constraints, such as determining when a person can get a driver's license, marry, vote, join the armed forces, or hold elective office.

There are also informal yet no less influential sets of social expectations that define the "right time," or the optimum period, to take on certain roles, to fulfill various functions, and to attain levels of accomplishment deemed desirable by society—or, more specifically, by that segment of society that constitutes your social niche. There are more or less standard times for completing one's education, getting married for the first time, becoming a parent or a grandparent, and reaching a certain level of seniority in one's job. These culturally defined timetables constitute a *social clock*. Having internalized this social clock, people generally try to adhere to its dictates, and think of themselves as "on time," "late," or "early" with respect to one or another life event. Matching the expectations of the social clock with the events of middle life exerts an important influence on our perception of how well our lives have progressed and what the future bodes for us.

Yet another dimension is *historical time*. Despite the basic commonalities of human existence, the life experiences of each generation are in some ways unique. To spend a significant portion of one's life in a country at war, for example, is very different from living in a time of peace, and each major experience differs in its effect according to one's age, sex, and other variables. This consideration has become particularly important in the twentieth century, which has witnessed more cataclysmic events on a worldwide scale and a faster pace of technological and social change than any comparable period in history. Those who are now in their fifties were born during the Depression and lived through the Second World War, the Korean War, the war in Vietnam, and other more localized upheavals. They have witnessed the enormous expansion of air travel, culminating in the exploration of space; the development of new means of communication, ranging from telephones to television to satellites; the harnessing of nuclear energy and the threat of global destruction through nuclear war; the computer revolution; the discovery of antibiotics and the birth control pill, along with the transplantation of organs and other biomedical advances.

Even though we may not fully understand the significance of a major innovation or event when it happens, it is safe to assume that each generation is likely to be marked by it. Hence the *cohort effect* is a significant confounding variable when we try to study life stages. For instance, if we examine the lives of a group of individuals in their fifties, do we ascribe a particular set of attitudes to their age, or to the fact that these men and women were adolescents during the second World War, or the parents of teenagers during the turbulent 1960s? To control for the cohort effect we would need to do numerous studies to identify what elements, if any, are characteristic of the age group as such other than the shared social circumstances of their lives. Those studies are yet to be done.

AGES AND STAGES

A human life, like a river, meanders through its course, rushing through rapids, flowing placidly over the plains, twisting and turning through countless bends until it spends itself. It is the same river; yet it looks very different from one place to another. So it is with our lives; circumstances vary from one time to another in the course of a life. To impose a semblance of order on this process, people have thought of life as consisting of ages and stages: hence the popular notion of a stepwise progression through life and the metaphor of life as a play with many acts.

The contrast between the immature young and the mature adult is so obvious that the distinction must have been apparent since time immemorial. Yet our present conception of childhood as a phase of life is actually only a few hundred years old. Children were dressed and treated as miniature adults throughout the Middle Ages. It was only during the seventeenth and eighteenth centuries that concern over their exploitation led to the perception of children as being categorically different from adults and of childhood as a distinct phase of life.

Similarly, although the changes of puberty are obvious, it was not until the turn of this century that the notion of adolescence, in terms that we now commonly understand, began to take shape. Napoleon was a captain at age 16, but he was not a teenager in the sense in which we now use the term. Hence, it is not biology alone but biology *and* culture that define these entities.

A similar process of redefinition is now taking place with respect to adulthood. Until recently, adulthood was perceived as a plateau that stretched from the end of adolescence to the beginning of old age. Now it is seen as a period with its own distinctive phases.

Daniel Levinson divides the adult years into "eras" that are joined by "transitional periods." Thus, the period of early adult transition (ages 17–22) ushers in the era of early adulthood (ages 22–40); the midlife transition (ages 40–45) leads to the era of middle adulthood (ages 45–60); and the late adult transition (ages 60–65) culminates in the late adult era (age 65 and over).[8] Others now distinguish between the "young-old" (ages 65–76) and the "old-old" (75 and above). As old age stretches on and is further differentiated, there may one day be a "middle-old" distinction as well.

Although Levinson does not claim that these ages constitute *precise* demarcations for all, other investigators are not sure that even *approximate* ages can be meaningfully applied to the process of adult development. The notion of life stages is itself far from generally accepted, even though it has had broad exposure and wide appeal in both the professional and popular literature. Erik Erikson, who more than anyone else has helped establish the concept of the life cycle, is very much a stage theorist.[9] Most popular books on this subject likewise follow a stage-oriented perspective.[10]

The appeal of the life-stages approach is not hard to understand. Subdividing life into more manageable segments conveys a sense of order and makes it easier to deal with its complexities. The concept of a succession of stages is akin to a blueprint or a road map; it predicts what landmarks one is likely to encounter in a given phase and thereby encourages the hope of better managing its vicissitudes.

The notion of life stages may be illusory, however, when applied to a period of midlife or some particular aspect of it such as the so-called "midlife crisis." As Orville Brim has stated,

> There is as yet no evidence either for developmental periods or "stages" in the mid-life period, in which one event must come after another, or one personality change brings another in its wake. The existence of "stages," if proved true, would be a powerful concept in studying mid-life; meanwhile there is a danger of our using this facile scheme as a cover for loose thinking about human development, without carrying forward the necessary hard-headed analyses of the evidence.[11]

STUDYING ADULT DEVELOPMENT

Despite sporadic attempts in the past to study developmental changes in adulthood, this phase of life has been largely neglected until recently. Although adults run the world and much of the literature of the world deals with their life experiences, the concept of *adulthood* as an explicitly defined developmental stage has taken a long time to evolve. It is only since the Second World War that the systematic study of adulthood has gathered momentum.

Adulthood is a hard subject to study, not only because adult life is long and complex, but also because change occurs slowly during this period. Physical change takes place rapidly during childhood and adolescence, and then again in old age. But the changes between age twenty and sixty are so much more gradual (except for the menopause) that one barely perceives them as they occur. The same is true in the psychosocial realm.

A number of basic themes pervade the professional literature on adult development. One is the theme of constancy versus change. To what extent does personality remain constant during adulthood? Are the changes that occur merely marginal, or do they significantly alter who we are? How is adult personality as a whole related to its antecedents in childhood and adolescence?[12]

Even if it were established that personality changes occur in adulthood, in order for such change to qualify as *development*, there must be a process whereby the organism is irreversibly transformed in an orderly way over a period of time, and this process must be generally evident. In other words, development signifies universality, permanence, and predictability. But whether or not a developmental process must always constitute a positive gain is more difficult to know. The changes that go on after we have attained adulthood, and which are part of the aging process, have been traditionally viewed in negative terms, whereby something is lost rather than gained. Those who are now studying adult development, however, consider both the positive and negative consequences of aging as part of the lifelong process of development.

What are the fundamental causes of constancy and change? While everyone agrees that both biological and social determinants are crucial for human development at any stage of life, and that interactional models are the most sensible, the question still remains as to whether biological or social determinants carry more weight. For example, biological changes at midlife impose certain realities upon female reproductive functions, but the psychological and social consequences of these biological changes are not fixed; they are determined by one's response to them.

The systematic study of adult development relies on one of two major approaches. *Cross-sectional* studies compare groups of individuals of different ages. To determine how aging affects memory, for example, a researcher may give the same tests to twenty-, fifty-, or seventy-year-olds and look for differences in performance. In *longitudinal studies,* the same group of subjects, all within a given age range, are studied periodically over a number of years.

Each of these approaches has its assets and its liabilities. Cross-sectional studies are much easier to conduct, as they can be carried out over a relatively short period of time. But they suffer from the uncertainties of comparing individuals who are different not only in age but possibly in other ways, such as educational level.

Longitudinal studies obviate some of these problems by dealing with the same individuals over time, thus isolating age as a discrete variable. But longitudinal studies have their own pitfalls. They are much more difficult to carry out, and those who start them rarely get to finish them. (George Vaillant, who wrote the latest report on the Grant study, was three years old when the study was conceived.)[13] Keeping track of subjects over many years is very difficult, and those who drop out not only reduce the size of the sample, but skew it as well. Life-span psychologists are now devising methods of resolving some of these difficulties.[14]

I have summarized these issues to alert you to the fact that the study of adult development is still in its infancy. Although it is growing rapidly, there are very few studies of any substance whose findings can be generally applied to the middle-aged population. The problem is particularly acute with respect to women. Dominant theories on personality development, especially those with a psychoanalytic slant, have been criticized for being based on observations of men's lives.[15] At the moment not enough is known to present an in-depth and coherent view of what it means for a woman to go through midlife. Nor is the data on men significantly more complete.

PLANNING FOR THE FUTURE

To budget your time when you don't know how much time you have is difficult. While some fifty-year-olds are going to die before they reach their next birthday, most are going to live much longer, perhaps for as long as three or more decades. To behave as if one is never going to die, however, is foolish. Everyone should therefore have a will and other legal documents in good order and should make whatever provisions are necessary to help their survivors carry on after they are gone. Anyone who has a responsible job should make comparable arrangements at work. If one has strong feelings about funerary arrangements, or the use of special medical procedures, these matters should be settled as far as possible. Once these basic necessities are taken care of, you can proceed on the assumption that you are going to be around for a long time.

Though retirement may be a decade or more away, some arrangements require a long lead time. It is a good idea to review the anticipated benefits of your retirement plan and ascertain your financial prospects so that you neither fall short when the time comes nor needlessly deprive yourself now by setting aside more than you are likely to need.

There has to be a balance between endlessly postponing what you want to do and rushing precipitously to do things that would be disruptive. If you have decided to see Antarctica, it will still be there, and you are likely to be alive, ten years from now. But then, if going to Antarctica can just as well be done now, why wait?

Time, like money, is best spent judiciously—neither pinched nor thrown away. But excessive consciousness of either process spoils your enjoyment. If drinking a thirty-dollar bottle of wine makes you feel guilty, don't drink it; if you must take the bread out of someone else's mouth in order to buy the wine, don't buy it. But once you've bought it, don't calculate what each sip is costing you.

During much of our lives, we spend our time and money with an eye to future consequences. As a fifty-year-old you can get out from under that burden. You have discharged your basic duties as a parent, you have put time and effort into establishing your career. From now on, you can do things more for their own sake, not for their instrumental value. You have saddled your horse—now ride it.

There is a fine line between too much and too little preparation for the future. Unfortunately, no one can tell you where to draw the line—only you can decide that—but I can assure you that the line will by necessity be arbitrary, and you must be prepared to adjust it as circumstances dictate.

Entering a new decade is like crossing a geographical boundary. When the journey of your life is smoothly moving from one stage to the next, aging is like passing a road sign telling motorists they are leaving one county or state and entering its neighbor. But more often the end of a decade is like leaving one country and entering another: We must stop, have our passport checked and luggage searched, answer questions about where we are going and why. There is some satisfaction in arriving at our destination, a certain sense of excitement in the very process of crossing the border. But more often there is the tedium of taking things out and then putting them back in place. And there is the nagging anxiety over not having with us what is required or having things that one is not supposed to carry.

In crossing into fifty, you are both passenger and customs agent, and how you conduct the exercise at the checkpoint is entirely up to you. If you know you are clean, go easy on yourself. But if you have been smuggling contraband across the previous boundaries of your life, this is a good time to turn your luggage inside out, come to terms with yourself and those around you, and get on with the rest of your journey.

There are those who think self-understanding adds insult to injury, but, as Socrates said, the unexamined life is not worth living. At age fifty there is still time to think through where you have been and where you are heading and to make some meaningful adjustments for the foreseeable future. There is still time to listen to all those muffled voices within you that are clamoring to be heard. Even if you cannot adjudicate all claims and settle all debts, you can still make some amends to yourself and to others. Then close old accounts; turn your eyes to the reality of today and the anticipation of tomorrow. But in doing so, do not get caught up in an obsessional loop—fighting over and over the lost battles of your life—or be embittered by the seemingly capricious turns of fate. More than ever before, age fifty is the time to eliminate excess baggage and start making the best of the rest of your life.

To that end, you need to care for your body, attend to your psychological needs and to the maintenance of your close relationships, manage your career, and prepare to deal with the adjustments that will be necessary in all of these areas. It is to these issues that we shall now turn.

2

THE
BODY
AT
50

The body at fifty: How does it look? How does it feel? How well does it work? Physical changes during midlife are part of the silent process of aging, a process that started at birth and will continue inexorably to the end of life. But what does it mean to age? Do people, like fruits and vegetables, ripen and rot as they grow older, or is there more to life than that?

Physical aging is a biological phenomenon that we share with other living organisms. But *getting old* as a psychological and social experience is uniquely human. The physical changes in midlife, in and of themselves, explain very little of the life experiences of being fifty. Much of what defines us as "middle-aged" men and women is culturally determined, even though the cultural reactions are responses to the real or imagined, present or anticipated consequences of growing old.

Turning fifty does not mean that your body inevitably goes to pot. For fifty-year-olds who are reasonably healthy and fit, the effect of aging on ordinary everyday physical functions is minimal. There is actually great variability among individuals in the timing and magnitude of physiological change. *Patterns* of aging apply to people in general but the *timing* of changes varies among individuals. Furthermore, although the general effect of aging is one of gradual physical decline, different body parts and functions decline at different rates. The body gradually loses its capacity for extreme exertion and peak performance, but not its ability to carry out the ordinary activities of life.

The condition of your body at fifty is therefore only partly determined by your age. Your ability to participate in any particular sport or to enjoy any physical activity is determined for the most part by your state of health and level of fitness. But in order to anticipate what is in store and to avoid imposing unnecessary burdens on the inevitable consequences of growing old, it is important to understand the process and the manifestations of aging.

Why do we grow old? The enigma of aging has been a source of fascination and trepidation since time immemorial. Aging, with its inevitable culmination in death, is central to the religious beliefs, myths, and traditions of all cultures. In Greek mythology, the Hyperboreans lived for a thousand years. In the Old Testament, Noah and Methuselah lived lives only somewhat shorter. The earliest Egyptian papyrus on aging dates back to about 1600 B.C. and deals with attempts to transform an old man into a youth. Aristotle hypothesized that all living organisms started life with a reserve of innate heat that was dissipated during the process of living. Greek medicine attributed aging to the imbalance of bodily humors, and Hippocrates recommended a moderate diet and regular exercise for longevity.

The scientific study of aging dates back to the turn of the century, but until the last few decades, attempts to understand the aging process were highly speculative. Today there are many theories that attempt to explain the mechanisms of senescence. While none of these theories is as yet accepted as definitive, some are deemed more plausible than others. The key issue is not why cells die; at any given moment millions of the cells of our body are dying and being replaced. The question is, Why do cells eventually cease to replicate themselves? The process of wear and tear affects tissues all the time, but with aging the capacity of the body to repair the damage becomes progressively less.

Ultimately the control process must be genetic and specific to a particular species, which is why some animals live longer than others. But the site and the mechanism of the "genetic clock" ticking away is as yet unclear. The limitation in the number of times that cells are capable of dividing may explain not only why we are mortal, but also the process of aging that leads to death.

Some theories assume various self-destruct mechanisms that eventually do us in. The autoimmune system, for instance, may with aging become less effective in identifying and combating harmful foreign bodies. Or its antibodies may fail to discriminate between foreign elements and the body's own tissues, and like soldiers gone berserk, turn their weapons against their own people. The free-radical theory of aging hypothesizes that highly reactive chemicals oxidize and slowly damage body tissues—as if "rusting" us from the inside. Or the aging process may be the result of cumulative random errors or mutations which garble the DNA codes essential for protein synthesis.[1]

However we look at it, all of these theories point to a naturally orchestrated planned obsolescence of the body. Unpleasant as this prospect may be at a personal level, life could hardly be otherwise. If the continued entry of new offspring into the world were not accompanied by the simultaneous exit of the aged, the earth would have long ago been overwhelmed. Life is therefore meaningless without the reality of death. It is no wonder that Adam and Eve became mortal when they discovered sexuality.

CHANGES IN APPEARANCE

By age fifty, most men and women manifest the beginnings of the alterations on the surface of their bodies that will eventually make them look old. But the psychological reactions and the symbolism of these superficial changes are far more significant than the changes themselves in determining a person's contentment with his or her self-image in midlife.

Wrinkles are wrinkles: For some they represent the fading of beauty and the loss of sexual attractiveness and potency; for others, they are "the long-service stripes earned in the hard campaign of life. A wrinkled face is a firm face, a steady face, a safe face. Wrinkles are the dried up riverbeds of a lifetime's tears. Wrinkles are the nostalgic remnants of a million smiles. Wrinkles are the crannies and footholds on the smooth visage of life to which any man can cling and gain some comfort and security."[2]

Gray Hair: The graying of hair is the quintessential sign of aging. The production of hair pigment slows down in adulthood. Strands of white hair are not uncommon in young adults, but the process becomes more marked in midlife.

The timing and patterning of graying hair is genetically determined, although environmental and emotional factors may also play a part. In some cultures, prematurely gray hair is equated with having suffered many hardships in life.

Baldness: The difference in the hairline of men and women is established during puberty under the influence of the male hormone testosterone. As a result, the male hairline recedes farther back than that of the female following puberty. This process becomes progressively more marked during the forties and fifties; 45 percent of men aged forty-five have significant degrees of baldness. Baldness is genetically controlled, but since the male hormone also plays a role, women are less susceptible to baldness than men.

Most middle-aged men take the graying of their hair and beards in stride, but they are more troubled by baldness. Graying temples are thought to make a man look distinguished, especially if he has already achieved status. (Graying does not improve the image of men standing in a breadline.) Gray hair is generally considered to be less becoming to middle-aged women, which is why so many dye their hair (as do a smaller proportion of men). This difference is part of the broader social discrepancy with which the process of aging is perceived among men and women and which places a disproportionate burden on women.

Wrinkles: Wrinkles are unlikely to be welcomed by either men or women, and there are no convenient ways of concealing them—or effective ways of preventing them. The appearance of the body surface is determined by the texture of the skin, its underlying layers of fat, and the deeper musculature. The process of aging affects all three; but, equally important, all three are also influenced by the effects of environmental factors, especially exposure to the sun because ultraviolet and "tanning rays" of the sun make the skin less elastic, and cigarette smoking because nicotine constricts blood vessels, thereby reducing the supply of oxygen and nutrients to the skin and slowing the elimination of waste products.

The skin is both the wrapping of the body and one of its largest organs, accounting for about 16 percent of body weight. It has several important functions: The skin protects the body from injury and drying, receives stimuli from the environment, excretes various substances, and takes part in temperature regulation and the maintenance of water balance.

The two main layers of the skin are the *epidermis*, which constitutes its surface, and the *dermis*, its deeper layer. The epidermis is covered by a protective coating of dead cells, which are shed sporadically. With aging, these cells tend to accumulate, giving the skin a coarser appearance.

The principal mass of dermis consists of *connective tissue*, which is composed of several types of *fibers*, and an amorphous gel called the *ground substance*. The fibers consist mainly of collagen and elastin, which provide the supportive and elastic meshwork of the skin. Within the dermis are embedded the hair follicles, the sweat glands, and the sebaceous glands, which produce a natural oily coating to keep the hair shafts and the skin moist and soft.

With aging, the skin glands become less efficient, causing a dryness that becomes particularly noticeable among older individuals (and predisposes their skin to itch). But dryness of the skin as such does not cause wrinkles. The process by which wrinkles are produced is more complex, having to do with structural changes in the meshwork of connective tissue that supports the skin. As the fibers in the dermis lose their elasticity, the supportive matrix is undermined, and the epidermis collapses along frown lines in the forehead and deeper grooves along the corners of the mouth. As a result, we get laugh lines, crow's feet, lip creases, and brow furrows, as well as finer wrinkling (the crepe-paper effect).

The configuration of facial wrinkles is to some extent determined by one's habitual facial expressions. Hence, the lines that mark the faces of mature adults reflect something of their personality and their dominant moods over the years. This is why an older face has more "character" than the bland, smooth faces of the young. As the famous designer Gabrielle "Coco" Chanel put it, "Nature gives you the face you have at twenty; it is up to you to merit the face you have at fifty."

Body Weight: Of the many factors contributing to the changing shape and figure of the middle-aged body, the most important, from a health perspective, is the tendency to gain weight. Typically, people will become progressively heavier until the age of fifty-five or so and then begin to lose weight gradually. The replacement of muscle mass with fat, along with the expanding midsection, gives the middle-aged their flabby appearance. ("Middle age," says Bob Hope, "is when your age starts to show around your middle.") This process is more marked among men, whose average body fat increases from 11 percent at age twenty to 30 percent by age sixty-five; among women the ratio of fat—close to 30 percent at age twenty—does not change significantly in the later years. A number of causes underlie this tendency to gain weight in the middle years—some metabolic, some dietary—but most important is the tendency to lead a more sedentary life.

CHANGES IN BODILY FUNCTIONS

While alterations in physical appearance manifest themselves through structural changes in the tissues of the body, changes are concurrently occurring in the internal structures and organs.[3] These do not start in middle age but are in progress throughout adult life—at different rates for different systems and in different individuals (see Figure 2-1). We are largely unaware of these slow internal transformations until their effects become manifest in disturbed functions.

Muscular Function: Maximum muscular strength is attained between the ages of twenty-five and thirty. Through exercise and proper nutrition, however, the bulk and density of muscles can be improved until middle age. Among older individuals, the number of active muscle fibers and their protein content begin to decrease, leading to a gradual decrease in the speed and force of muscular contractions and in the capacity to sustain muscular effort. The muscles of the

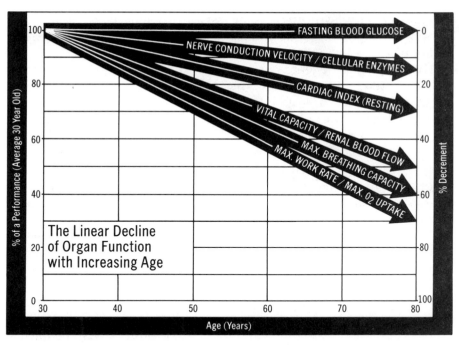

The graph labeled "The Linear Decline of Organ Function with Increasing Age" with y-axis "% of a Performance (Average 30 Year Old)" from 0 to 100, right axis "% Decrement" from 0 to 100, x-axis "Age (Years)" from 30 to 80. Lines shown: FASTING BLOOD GLUCOSE, NERVE CONDUCTION VELOCITY / CELLULAR ENZYMES, CARDIAC INDEX (RESTING), VITAL CAPACITY / RENAL BLOOD FLOW, MAX. BREATHING CAPACITY, MAX. WORK RATE / MAX. O₂ UPTAKE.

FIGURE 2-1. Note that the loss of performance capacity varies widely in different systems. The ability to maintain the blood glucose levels does not change at all; nerve conduction velocity changes relatively little, while the maximum work rate declines sharply.

back are particularly vulnerable to this change; in the early fifties, the strength of the back is down to about 90 percent of its maximum level, and declines rapidly thereafter. But so far as other muscle clusters (such as the arm and shoulder) are concerned, the sharp drop in a man's strength does not set in until well into the sixth decade. Although women also experience a decline in strength, they are less likely to feel incapacitated unless they have engaged in the sort of heavy labor or recreational exertion more typical of men.

Various components of connective tissue support the skin, sustain muscle fibers, and connect them to bones through ligaments. Alterations in connective tissue throughout the body are among the most important manifestations of the aging process and play a central role in the illnesses (such as arthritis) that plague millions of older individuals. With aging, an increase in the density of collagen results in a thickening of connective tissue and a consequent loss of elasticity, so that joints become stiffer and their movements more restricted.

Bones and Joints: In half the middle-aged population, x-rays disclose degenerative changes in the joints, but less than half of those persons experience any symptoms. The basic problem is osteoarthritis, caused by the wearing out of the pad of cartilage interposed between the two bony surfaces of a joint.

The process of degeneration starts with a roughening and fraying of the cartilage surface. Since the reparative process whereby lost cartilage is replaced is now less effective, a progressive net loss of cartilage occurs over time. Inflammatory changes and alterations in the bone itself may be superimposed on this process.

The Heart and Lungs: The heart muscle itself does not change significantly with aging, especially if the person remains physically active, but by the mid-fifties the heart rate becomes slower and more irregular. The pumping action of the heart does not generate the same level of cardiac output as it did in younger years.

Thickening of the walls of the minute air sacs in the lungs begins to hinder the diffusion of oxygen into the bloodstream. The passage of oxygen from the blood to the working muscles is in turn hindered by the thickening of the sheets of connective tissue that surround the muscle fibers. Since the fine capillary blood vessels are buried in this connective tissue, it becomes more difficult for oxygen and nutrients to pass into the muscle fibers and for waste products from the muscle fibers to flow back into the bloodstream.

Simultaneously, the amount of work that muscles can do for a limited period of time without an adequate supply of oxygen (or the extent to which they can incur an "oxygen debt") is sharply reduced, decreasing as much as 60 percent between the ages of twenty and fifty. The amount of oxygen that the blood can carry remains fairly stable until age fifty and then begins to decline.

All of this may seem to imply severe physical limitations for the middle-aged person. Fortunately that is not the case. In a healthy and active fifty-year-old what is lost is only the capacity for peak performance. Fifty-year-old athletes cannot win over trained competitors half their age, but they can easily outperform the great majority of ordinary people of any age. Because the condition of the body is more important than age, Jane Fonda can say in midlife, "I can run farther, stretch deeper, climb steeper, lift heavier, stand taller, and dance longer than when I was twenty."[4]

One way of getting around the handicap of age is through more frequent periods of rest. Even though the older person has more difficulty in sustaining physical effort and takes longer to recover from it, one can still walk, run, swim, or ski for long distances by doing it in shorter stretches punctuated by rest periods.

Certain changes in the cardiovascular system have a more direct impact on health and longevity. The coronary arteries that supply blood to the muscle of the heart become somewhat narrowed even in apparently healthy individuals between the ages of forty and fifty. Electrocardiograms show that the efficiency of the heart during exercise is diminished because of its decreasing ability to supply blood for its own use as well as to the rest of the body. These changes in themselves do not constitute heart disease but rather represent a heightened vulnerability to such conditions as the individual enters middle age.

Other changes in the peripheral vascular system result in a progressive rise in blood pressure in the fifth and sixth decades. Blood pressure, which is low in childhood, registers its first sharp increase during adolescence and the next one after age fifty. The progressive rise in blood pressure becomes an illness only when other factors push it up to pathological levels.

CHANGES IN SENSORY FUNCTION

Vision: The lens of the eye loses some of its elasticity over time, and one's best viewing distance lengthens progressively, so that by age fifty most people have to use reading glasses or hold the reading material farther away. Some, however, may have a problem with distant vision. The diameter of the pupil tends to decrease so that middle-aged and older people have more difficulty in dimly lit places like theaters and restaurants, even though they may have perfectly good vision otherwise. Driving at night becomes more difficult because recovery from glare and adaptation to the dark take longer.

Hearing: Hearing acuity, like visual acuity, is at its peak at about age twenty, after which it gradually diminishes, more so for higher than for lower tones. Most middle-aged individuals are not aware of this gradual loss since it does not affect their everyday life. It is usually not until their seventies that people begin to miss words in conversation. Hearing loss is greater for men than for women, possibly because more men are exposed to excessive noise in work settings; and for some reason the left ear seems more likely to be affected than the right.

Taste: The typical fifty-year-old has no problem in discriminating the four basic tastes (sweet, sour, salt, and bitter), but may become less aware of more subtle gastronomic distinctions. This does not become a problem until old age: When food appears to lose its taste, the elderly are more likely to experience eating problems.

Touch: Sensitivity to touch begins to decline at about age forty-five and to pain at about age fifty, but the tolerance for pain decreases simultaneously, so that pain causes greater distress for older individuals.

CHANGES IN SLEEP PATTERNS

Changes in the central nervous system may be responsible for alterations in sleep patterns. Contrary to the common belief that the older one gets the less sleep one needs, the total number of hours people sleep per night generally remains about the same (about seven hours) as does the amount of rapid eye movement (REM) sleep, which accompanies dreaming. With increasing age, however, one tends to wake up oftener during the night and hence get less of the deeper kind of sleep. Middle-aged and older individuals often spend more hours lying awake and therefore feel less rested in the morning than younger individuals.

CHANGES IN REPRODUCTIVE FUNCTION

More misconceptions surround midlife changes in reproductive and sexual functions than any other bodily system. We shall deal with sexual functions in the next chapter and focus here mainly on ovarian function in women and testicular function in men.

The Menopause: The menopause, or the climacteric (which means "rung of a ladder" in Greek), is a predictable, universal, and normal occurrence that all women experience, usually between the late forties and the early fifties. It is characterized by the loss of reproductive capacity in women, but it is a "loss" over which no one needs to shed tears. Long before they reach fifty, most women gladly give up childbearing.

The menstrual cycle goes on with more or less regularity over the three decades of a woman's fertile life. Then in the mid-forties the process becomes erratic, and by the early fifties it ends just as mysteriously as it started. The organs responsible for the cessation of the menstrual process are the ovaries. Hypothalamic and pituitary hormones continue to be produced but no longer stimulate any response from the ovaries. The result is a sharp drop in the production of the female hormones—estrogens and progestins.

Lack of menstrual periods usually signifies the absence of ovulation, but a woman may continue to ovulate even while skipping periods. If she has stopped using contraceptives and assumed that she is no longer fertile, she may be startled to find herself pregnant. The rhythm method of birth control is particularly unreliable at these times because of irregular cycles. Women should therefore use a reliable birth control method for a full year after their last period if they want to avoid becoming pregnant.

All of the symptoms of the menopause are due to the sharp drop (to one-tenth their normal values) of the hormones produced by the ovaries. The vaginal lining gradually becomes thinner, vaginal secretions decrease, and the lubricatory response during sexual arousal becomes less profuse. Changes occur in the breasts, which become smaller and less firm, and in the subcutaneous layers of bodily fat, so that significant transformations in the shape of the female body result. These changes begin to be noticeable during the menopause, but many years pass before their full effects become evident.

The menopause is not a disease and the severity of its manifestations varies widely. Discussion of the symptoms of the menopause need to be freed from bias and insensitivity. It is not necessary either to exaggerate or to deny their significance. About one out of four women will experience virtually no discomfort during this period; others will experience one or more troublesome symptoms, but only a minority will have a hard time. There are now safe and effective ways of providing hormonal replacement so that a great many of these disturbing symptoms can be prevented or significantly ameliorated. The following description of symptoms must be understood in that context.

The most distinctive physical manifestation of the menopause is the hot flash (or hot flush). Experienced by two out of three women, this symptom may range from a barely noticeable sensation of warmth to an intense feeling of heat that sweeps over the upper chest, neck, and face, with or without sweating and chills. They may last a few seconds or several minutes; they may come once a month or ten or twenty times a day. They may occur at any time of the day or night. In some cases they are triggered by emotional upsets or alcohol. Hot flashes usually persist over a year or two with decreasing frequency. In rare cases, a woman may continue having them into her sixties.

Other complaints that are harder to document are changes in memory and concentration. These are usually no worse than momentary forgetfulness but may provoke anxiety if women associate them with the onset of old age. Joint and muscle pains trouble about one out of four women. Usually the small joints of the fingers are involved but the back and the neck also may be affected. A related difficulty is a sense of unsteadiness and a fear of falling.

Osteoporosis ("porous bones"), which makes bones more fragile, affects some 20 million postmenopausal women in the United States. Though the process starts in the mid-thirties, it becomes accelerated when the drop in estrogens makes bones less able to retain calcium. This process can be counteracted, if not entirely prevented, by the administration of estrogens and calcium, as well as through proper nutrition and exercise.

Other minor but irritating symptoms affect the aging skin, which bruises more easily, feels dry, and may develop itching, burning, and tingling sensations, sometimes described as "ants crawling under the skin." Partly because of these sensations, women become more sensitive to being touched. They may find that even the sensation of tight clothing on their skin is unpleasant, and they feel most comfortable in a loose nightgown or robe. Severe cases extend to downright aversion to being touched by others, including husbands. These changes are thought to be due to alterations in nerve impulse transmission, but they may also have psychological components.

Other psychological states include moodiness and transient periods of sadness. Depression is not an inevitable consequence of the menopause, but in some cases serious depressive episodes have their onset at this time. More typically, the onslaught of these physical sensations along with psychological concerns produce a sense of "fragility," which makes some women feel vulnerable and leads to social withdrawal. They may be reluctant to leave the house, which in some cases takes on the forbidding proportions of a phobia.

Male Climacteric: Is there a "male menopause"? Over the last several decades some researchers have suggested that men undergo a process similar to the menopause in women. Although some investigators continue to ascribe the fatigue, irritability, and lack of concentration experienced by middle-aged men to a hormonal process, the dominant view is that there is no such thing as a male climacteric.

Many middle-aged men go through a "midlife crisis," but that constellation of psychological reactions (discussed in subsequent chapters) is a response to occupational and other life situations rather than to hormonal changes. The production of sex hormones (testosterone) in the male may decline very gradually with age, but only in rare instances is there a drop in testosterone production so sharp that it causes men to experience hot flashes similar to those of menopausal women. In the normal course of events a man continues to produce sperm and testosterone, albeit in progressively smaller quantities, so that he remains fertile into old age.

ILLNESS AND DISABILITY
IN MIDLIFE

The manifestations of aging are a normal part of life, however disabling they may eventually become. Illness is a pathological condition superimposed on this developmental process; yet this distinction is not easy to maintain. For example, the changes in connective tissue can be conceived both as part of the normative process of aging (such as wrinkle formation) and as the underlying cause of certain forms of illness (such as arthritis). Furthermore, aging increases the likelihood of cardiovascular disorders, cancer, and various other chronic conditions.

There are now enough elderly people in good health among us to reassure the middle-aged that getting old is not synonymous with becoming ill and disabled. Improved medical care has played a significant role in keeping people healthier in their older years, but a great deal of responsibility also rests on the individual. It is particularly important, therefore, for those entering the fifth decade to know how to enhance the chances of a long and healthy life. Prevention rather than reliance on cure must be the order of the day since, as the years go on, what gets broken becomes increasingly hard to fix.

Aging entails a gradual reduction in the capacity of organs to respond to internal and external challenges, the corollary of which is a progressive inefficiency in maintaining the homeostatic balance of the body. When pushed beyond the limit of its compensatory mechanisms, a system will break down. This fact is of great importance with respect to the cardiovascular system, since its diseases constitute the most common causes of disability and death in the middle years.

If the flow of blood is significantly impeded, the tissues that are deprived of oxygen and nutrients will malfunction and die. The process that most seriously compromises the blood flow is *atherosclerosis*. Atherosclerosis must be differentiated from *arteriosclerosis* or the "hardening" of arterial walls (although the two processes may coexist). Arteriosclerotic changes are concentric (involving the entire ring of a blood vessel) and diffuse (affecting a large portion of the arterial system). Atherosclerotic lesions are eccentric (located on part of a blood vessel only) and local (blocking only part of an artery). Arteriosclerosis typically causes hypertension (since hardened arteries produce more resistance to the blood flow). Atherosclerosis causes blockage at a particular site, or bleeding into the wall of the artery, which causes a swelling (aneurism) and possible rupture of the vessel.

Atherosclerotic changes have been noted in the blood vessels of Egyptian mummies—so the problem has been around for a long time. Although the process starts quite early in life, it does not usually begin to cause symptoms until the late forties. The oxygen deficiency may be transient; for example, when increased demand for oxygen (due to exertion, cold, or other factors) cannot be met by narrower coronary arteries, the person experiences an anginal attack with chest pain but usually no permanent damage. In the extremities, the decreased arterial flow causes severe pain, which usually subsides with rest. A blocked coronary artery results in a heart attack; a blocked cerebral artery causes a stroke; in the extremities, the result is gangrene. These are the usual but not inevitable outcomes of arterial blockage.

The consequences of atherosclerosis are clear but its causes are not. We know a good deal, however, about the *risk factors* that predispose some more than others to develop this condition (see Figure 2-2), but collectively, the known risk factors account for only 50 percent of the variance. Some of these factors cannot be altered, but those that can be modified allow considerable opportunity for preventive measures.

The risk of myocardial infarction increases with age regardless of sex. Gender is also an important variable in itself. Until age fifty, women lag ten to fifteen years behind men in showing the effects of atherosclerosis in their coronary, cerebral, and peripheral blood flow. Following the menopause, women begin to catch up with men. This increase may be due to the sharp drop in female hormones, which leaves the effect of testosterone in the female body unopposed (hence making the female body more like that of the male). It is also possible that the more vulnerable males having been eliminated by now, the net effect is one of a male population less at risk, rather than a female population more at risk.

Hypertension of even moderate proportions increases fivefold the risk of coronary heart disease, the strongest risk factor among those

Prevalence of Risk Factors in Cardiovascular Diseases Among the Middle-Aged

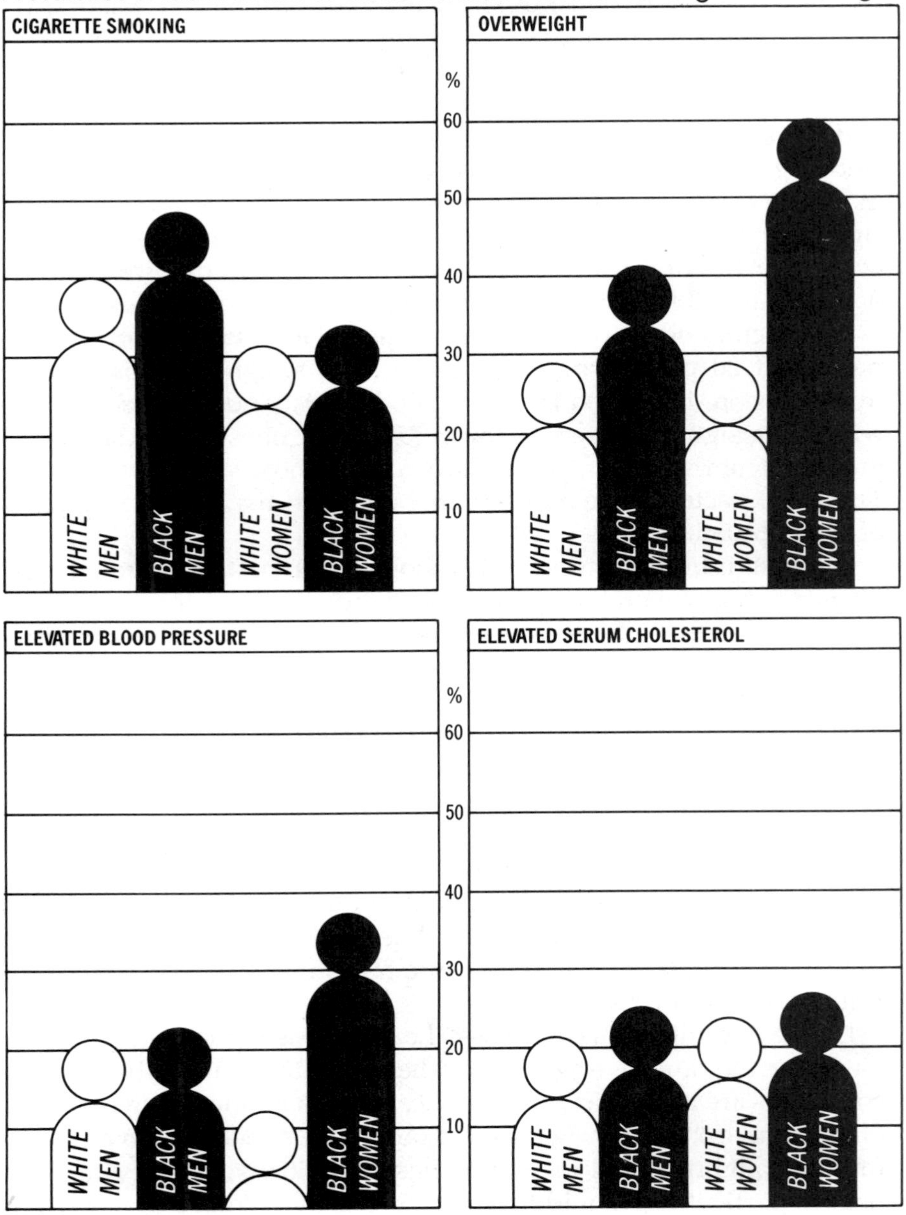

FIGURE 2-2.

older than forty-five—and also the likelihood of suffering a stroke. Another major risk is caused by the presence of high levels of lipids, particularly cholesterol and triglycerides, in the bloodstream. This risk is largely, although not exclusively, due to dietary factors, including high consumption of saturated fat, refined sugar, and total calories, especially by people whose life habits are sedentary.

Cigarette smoking increases by 70 percent the risk of heart attack and stroke among men at age forty-five; among women the effect of smoking is mainly an increase in the prevalence of arterial spasms in the legs. The severity of these changes is related to the number of cigarettes smoked. Giving up smoking sharply reduces the risks, even after the first heart attack. Cigar and pipe smokers are in less danger but still face significantly higher risks than nonsmokers.

Risk factors often work in conjunction. For instance, obesity, especially if 20 percent or more above ideal weight, predisposes to hypertension, increased levels of blood lipids, and diabetes, each of which is a significant risk factor in itself. But obesity also acts as an independent risk factor, particularly among those younger than fifty. These risk factors have a differential effect on the various segments of the population.

Other significant factors are psychological in nature. During recent years much attention has been focused on so-called Type A behavior, characterized by high levels of aggressiveness, ambition, competitive drive, and sense of time urgency, compared to the more relaxed behavior of the Type B person. Although the exact nature and significance of Type A behavior is currently in doubt, certain forms of stress continue to be suspect as significant factors in heart disease.

Cardiovascular disease and cancer are by far the most common causes of death in middle age and older years. Their prevalence increases while the frequency of other major causes of death, such as accidents, decreases compared to the younger years. Since the turn of the century, chronic conditions like cardiovascular diseases and cancer have replaced the more acute and infectious illnesses as the primary causes of death.

Unlike the infectious diseases, heart disease and cancer do not have discrete causative agents. Furthermore, these and other chronic conditions are related in very significant ways to how we live and the kind of environment we create for ourselves. Since we have not yet found straightforward cures for these conditions, the key to good health, particularly in middle age, is prevention. While prevention is important for the younger individual, it is a critical necessity for the middle-aged. With declining reserves and a progressively reduced capacity to recuperate, the middle and older years are no time for reckless disregard for the maintenance of the body. On the other hand, men and women in midlife have an unprecedented opportunity today to live out the remaining years of their lives in good health and vigor.

CARE AND MAINTENANCE
OF THE BODY

You now have fewer reserves to draw on; the recuperative power of your machinery is not what it used to be; and the process of gradual decline that you must contend with over the next several decades will become accelerated if you neglect the care and maintenance the body requires. On the positive side, personal initiative and diligence are likely to make a significant difference in the condition and performance of your body in midlife.

Skin and Cosmetics: When you are young it may not make much difference if you wear faded denim and do not comb your hair. In middle age, being unkempt is no longer charming.

At midlife people tend to practice good grooming and try to delay the normal changes of aging. But every wrinkle, every blemish need not be tackled head on with everything the cosmetics industry eagerly offers and with every hope medical science holds out. Such pointless preoccupation with the gradually aging body can cause much grief, and the narcissism that fuels it may turn to self-loathing.

Heredity is the strongest determinant of how your skin will age. For instance, those with thin, fair, dry skin and light eyes are more predisposed to wrinkling than those with darker and oilier skin and dark eyes. Nonetheless, premature and excessive wrinkling may be warded off by several measures.

Foremost among environmental causes is exposure to the sun. If you compare the texture of your sheltered buttocks with the exposed skin of your face and neck, you will see for yourself what the sun does to your skin. Since few of us are willing to sacrifice the pleasure of being outdoors, the most we can hope for is to avoid excessive exposure. There is no such thing as a "healthy" tan and one must use an effective sunscreen (with a factor rating of 15 or better) when exposure to the sun is prolonged, as it is at the beach or on the ski slopes. It is also a good idea to wear dark glasses to minimize squinting (which wrinkles the skin around the eyes) and to protect the eyes.

Smoking adds up to ten years to the appearance of your skin, as does a sedentary life-style. By contrast, vigorous exercise helps prevent wrinkling by increasing blood flow to the skin, eliminating wastes through sweating, fostering collagen production, reducing frowning by relieving stress, and avoiding repeated cycles of weight gain and loss that result in a slackening of the skin.

A well-balanced diet rich in vegetables and fruits and plenty of fluids (up to eight glasses of clear fluids a day) will help to preserve the skin. Alcohol and caffeine-containing beverages have a negative impact on the skin.

THE UNEQUAL BURDEN

Women resist the effects of age better than men in terms of health and life span. But when it comes to physical appearance, aging takes a greater toll on women than on men with respect to our cultural ideals of beauty and sexual attractiveness. This is particularly true for the changes at midlife.

Much is changing in this respect, however. Women, particularly in the middle class, now retain their looks longer than ever before. As a result of better health, fitness and grooming, they look decades younger than their contemporaries in the poverty stricken parts of the world.

The fear of lessening physical attractiveness nevertheless continues to preoccupy many women in midlife. Usually more conscious than men of the effects of aging on their appearance, women exert greater efforts to counteract and conceal them. On the other hand, resistance to this socially engrained pattern is growing.

Simone de Beauvoir, writing in *Force of Circumstance*, saw old age as "watching and waiting."

> I had the impression once of caring very little what sort of figure I cut. In much the same way, people who enjoy good health and always have enough to eat never give their stomachs a thought. While I was able to look at my face without displeasure

There are many ways of retaining and projecting an attractive image with individuality and good taste. Should people dye their hair? It depends. Gray hair is more becoming to some than to others. A wrinkled face blends naturally with gray hair; obviously dyed hair clashes with it. Similar considerations apply to whether a balding man should get a hairpiece or hair transplant. When pushed to a choice, it is better to look old than odd.

Cosmetics manufacturers produce a bewildering variety of lotions aimed at preventing, retarding, and diminishing wrinkles; these include repairers, renewers, cellular recovery complexes, and anti-ag-

---

I gave it no thought, it could look after itself. The wheel eventually stops. I loathe my appearance now: the eyebrows slipping down toward the eyes, the bags underneath, the excessive fullness of the cheeks, and that air of sadness around the mouth that wrinkles always bring. Perhaps the people I pass in the street see merely a woman in her fifties who simply looks her age, no more, no less. But when I look, I see my face as it was, attacked by the pox of time for which there is no cure.*

Germaine Greer, "can't pretend it's easy aging," but she sees the changes of midlife as an occasion for gaining freedom rather than fighting a rearguard battle.

Now, at last, we can escape from the self-consciousness of glamour; we can really listen to what people are saying, without worrying whether we look pretty doing it. . . . Some might say I am letting myself go. To a lifelong libertarian, that's a compliment. We ought to be turning ourselves loose, freeing ourselves from inauthentic ideas of beauty, from discomfort borne in order to be beautiful.**

* Simone de Beauvoir, *Force of Circumstance*, translated by Richard Howard (New York: G.P. Putnam's Sons, 1964), p. 656.
** G. Greer, "Letting Go," *Vogue*, vol. 176, no. 5 (May, 1986): 141–143.

ing complexes. If regulatory agencies allowed them, cosmeticians would make even bolder claims, though as yet no cosmetics have proven capable of preventing or permanently removing wrinkles.

The use of cosmetics can minimize some of the effects of the aging process and delay others. Most products containing exotic ingredients such as royal jelly, placental extract, turtle oil, mink oil, and natural proteins are usually quite safe to use, but they do not rejuvenate aged skin. They do more or less what good cold creams or vanishing creams do. Such emollients temporarily make fine surface lines less prominent, and they supply oil and moisture to combat the dryness and roughness of aging skin.

Moisturizers temporarily smooth finer wrinkles because the dry cells on the surface of the skin absorb moisture and swell up, thus making the skin look plump. More sophisticated products (called *humectants*) actually trap moisture within the skin layers through a chemical reaction. Cosmetics have no significant effect, however, on the deeper wrinkles that groove the face. Only surgical procedures can deal with those.

The cleansing of the skin with lotions or gentle abrasives removes the dead layers of the epidermis. This is more effectively accomplished by chemo-surgery (involving the use of powerful chemicals under general anesthesia). Such "peeling" of the skin does have some effect on very fine wrinkles because the mild transient swelling of the skin lasts for several months, but the procedure is painful and not free of risks. Like dermabrasion (which grinds the skin down), it is more appropriately used to correct scarring due to acne than to remove wrinkles. Facial masques of wax, clay, or plastic gel used by cosmeticians are not always safe and may cause harm by further stretching the skin when the masque is pulled off. Other measures, such as the application of hormone creams, injections of fetal cells, laser treatments, electrical stimulation, acupuncture, large doses of vitamins and minerals, and numerous other proposed remedies are of no demonstrable value.

A variety of surgical measures can be performed to deal with the deeper creases, but they do not help with fine wrinkles over large surfaces. Injection of collagen, a procedure that can be done in a doctor's office, can fill out the furrows between the nose and mouth and forehead lines. But the most effective way of eliminating wrinkles is through face-lifts (rhytidectomy). To predict the effect of such surgery, gently pull back the skin on your face in the areas that are most heavily wrinkled. Your mirror will tell you more or less how you will look if the surgery is successful. Face-lifts are not for everyone, not always successful, and not free of risks; nor will they prevent the appearance of new wrinkles. But in specific cases, a face-lift may create a marked improvement in one's appearance and, equally important, in the subjective perception of one's self.[5]

Diet and Weight Control: Whether or not an ample figure improves or detracts from your looks depends on your cultural background, social class, and the judgment of those whose aesthetic opinions you value. The rich are thinner in the Western world, and so far as the Duchess of Windsor was concerned, "No one could ever be too thin or too rich." Be that as it may, being overweight is not good for your health whatever your aesthetic or social ambitions.

In 1983 the Metropolitan Life Insurance Company revised its weight tables upward (see Figure 2-3). And more recently, based on data charted by twenty-five insurance companies, investigators at the Gerontology Research Center of the National Institute of Aging concluded that people in their fifties and sixties can afford to be somewhat heavier than even the upwardly revised Metropolitan Life charts indicate. Yet the American Heart Association and other authorities find the new Metropolitan Life figures too lenient and consider weights that are 20 percent higher than those figures to be hazardous; at that point being "overweight" crosses into being "obese" (no one is "fat" anymore).

There are two obvious aspects to eating—what you eat and how much you eat. Although the causes of obesity are complex and cannot be simply reduced to an arithmetical balance between caloric intake and consumption, excess food and a sedentary style of life have become the bane of affluent societies, particularly the United States. As a result, a substantial segment of the middle-aged, middle-class population is in a perpetual struggle to shed excess pounds.

There are many legitimate and effective diets designed to deal with various medical conditions. But you should place less trust in the popular diets that seem to come and go continuously. If they really worked, there would be no need for so many new alternatives. These popular diets may allow one to lose weight, but they rarely lead to a stable and workable dietary regimen that one can stay with day in and day out. As Jane Brody advises, "Don't go on any diet that you couldn't, wouldn't and shouldn't stay on for the rest of your life."[6]

I like good food and good wine, yet I have never been on a "diet" and have no difficulty controlling my weight by modulating how much I eat and selectively reducing or eliminating various items from

Desirable
Weight
Tables

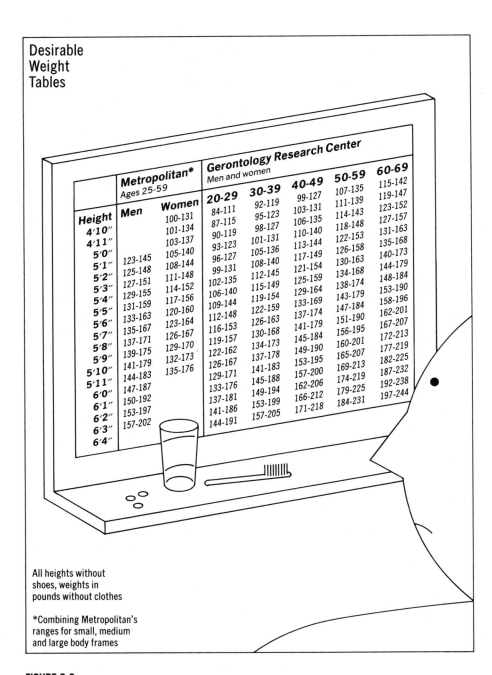

Height	Metropolitan* Ages 25-59 Men	Metropolitan* Ages 25-59 Women	Gerontology Research Center Men and women 20-29	30-39	40-49	50-59	60-69
4'10"		100-131	84-111	92-119	99-127	107-135	115-142
4'11"		101-134	87-115	95-123	103-131	111-139	119-147
5'0"		103-137	90-119	98-127	106-135	114-143	123-152
5'1"	123-145	105-140	93-123	101-131	110-140	118-148	127-157
5'2"	125-148	108-144	96-127	105-136	113-144	122-153	131-163
5'3"	127-151	111-148	99-131	108-140	117-149	126-158	135-168
5'4"	129-155	114-152	102-135	112-145	121-154	130-163	140-173
5'5"	131-159	117-156	106-140	115-149	125-159	134-168	144-179
5'6"	133-163	120-160	109-144	119-154	129-164	138-174	148-184
5'7"	135-167	123-164	112-148	122-159	133-169	143-179	153-190
5'8"	137-171	126-167	116-153	126-163	137-174	147-184	158-196
5'9"	139-175	129-170	119-157	130-168	141-179	151-190	162-201
5'10"	141-179	132-173	122-162	134-173	145-184	156-195	167-207
5'11"	144-183	135-176	126-167	137-178	149-190	160-201	172-213
6'0"	147-187		129-171	141-183	153-195	165-207	177-219
6'1"	150-192		133-176	145-188	157-200	169-213	182-225
6'2"	153-197		137-181	149-194	162-206	174-219	187-232
6'3"	157-202		141-186	153-199	166-212	179-225	192-238
6'4"			144-191	157-205	171-218	184-231	197-244

All heights without
shoes, weights in
pounds without clothes

*Combining Metropolitan's
ranges for small, medium
and large body frames

FIGURE 2-3.

time to time. This practice requires no calorie counting, no special food preparation, no fretting, and no fuss. Most important, my success in controlling my weight is directly linked to my ability to remain physically active.

Eating is one of the basic pleasures in life and is sustained by long-standing habits that are hard to change. The young and the old may suffer from malnutrition (because of food fads, faulty eating habits, ignorance, or poverty), but nutritional deficiency is not a problem for the middle-aged, although they tend to eat too much of the wrong kind of food.

By now, even hermits must have heard that Americans consume too much sugar, salt, red meat, fat, and cholesterol. Over 50 percent of our caloric intake is supplied by fat—compared to 10 percent in cultures with a very low incidence of obesity, heart attack, and stroke. Beyond satisfying your nutritional needs, the less fat you eat the better; and the smaller the proportion of saturated fats in what you eat, better still. Rely more on fats that are not solid (like butter) but liquid at room temperature; on oils that come from plants (especially olive and safflower oil) rather than animals; and consume the "white" meats of fish, chicken (without the skin), and veal, rather than beef (especially if marbled with fat).

To help prevent atherosclerosis you should reduce body weight to the optimal level; decrease the consumption of saturated fat to 30 percent of your caloric intake (with no more than 8 percent of the saturated variety); decrease the intake of cholesterol (which means restricting egg yolks and organ meats); restrict alcohol intake (a source of calories that also dramatically increases the secretion of low-density lipoproteins, which in turn raises the risk of coronary disease). High consumption of fat is also correlated with increased incidence of cancer of the breast, colon, and prostate gland. Increased fiber in the diet may play a role in reducing the risk of cancer of the bowel. Exposure of meats to high temperatures and smoke (as in charcoal broiling) may increase the formation of compounds with carcinogenic potential. Nitrites and nitrates (used in food preservatives and fertilizers) may pose a similar problem. Prudence would suggest limiting their consumption.

To reduce the risk of hypertension, salt intake should be controlled. For those with normal blood pressure, the use of salt is less significant than for those who are hypertensive or have relatives with high blood pressure. Most people merely need to moderate rather than drastically cut their salt intake.

Exercise and Fitness: Exercise combined with even modest attention to diet will maintain proper weight more easily than diet alone. There are a number of physiological and psychological reasons for this. The burning of calories through exercise is the most obvious but by no means the most important factor. It takes a good deal of strenuous exertion to make a dent in your store of fat. But the benefits of exercise are not restricted to the time in which you are actually exercising; exercise raises the metabolic rate of the body and the higher rate persists for a while after you stop (for how long is not yet known).

Think of the musculature of the body as constituting its locomotor engine. The more muscle, the bigger the engine; the more you use it, the higher the rate of calorie consumption. When you diet without exercise, the weight you lose is both fat and muscle. Your body now has a smaller "engine," and a lower consumption rate of caloric fuel. It also has a lower basal metabolic rate (or idling speed, as it were), which further cuts down caloric consumption. In other words, as you starve yourself your body reacts to protect itself by conserving its sources of energy, which works at cross-purposes to what you are trying to achieve. When you exercise regularly, you build up your muscle mass, thus increasing its "horsepower" and its rate of fuel consumption. Athletes can consume five times the number of calories recommended for a sedentary person, yet maintain their ideal weight.

The health benefits of exercise go beyond weight control. As the carbohydrate (glycogen) stored in muscle is depleted to provide energy, it is replenished by the uptake of glucose from the blood. Endurance exercise training also has an insulin-sparing effect, which may further reduce the insulin deficiency (hence the risk of diabetes) that tends to develop with increasing age. The loss of calcium and other minerals from bone (osteoporosis) that comes with aging is accelerated by inactivity (especially bed rest). This loss is especially significant for postmenopausal women, who are more likely to suffer the consequences of these changes, such as fractures. While exercise will not completely prevent bones from becoming more brittle, it is one of the most effective and safe ways of minimizing these effects. Most important, it has been repeatedly suggested (though not conclusively proven) that men and women who engage in physically more active jobs or leisure-time pursuits tend to experience fewer and less serious cardiovascular problems, such as coronary heart disease.

There is, at last, good evidence that regular exercise is a critical factor in promoting longevity. The optimum expenditure of energy through exercise is about 3500 calories per week—six to eight hours of strenuous exercise such as bicycling or singles tennis. Men who work out that much reduce by 50 percent the risk of death applicable to those who do little or no exercise; men who walk nine or more miles a week have a 21 percent lower risk of death than those who walk less than three miles. Furthermore, these are not all-or-none propositions. Even lower levels of exercise will reduce the death rate, though the reduction will be proportionately less (see Figure 2-4).

The psychological benefits of exercise are no less important. Physically active people report less anxiety and depression, more self-confidence, and greater ability to cope with stress—psychological effects powerful enough to cause some to become "addicted" to activities like running.

To produce these health benefits, exercise must be rigorous, systematic, and habitual enough to increase the body's working capacity or *physical fitness*. The benefits are a direct result of the increased metabolism required to supply energy to muscles, so that the most effective exercise consists of the rhythmic contractions of large muscles that occur in walking, hiking, jogging, running, cycling, skiing, swimming, and other active games and sports, as well as through vigorous exertion in housekeeping and physical labor.

During this level of exercise the metabolism of high energy compounds in muscle tissue takes place for the most part in the presence of oxygen, which explains why such exercise has come to be known as *aerobic*. If the intensity of exercise is greater than the level of exertion ordinarily undertaken by the individual, a significant rise in heart rate and breathing results with beneficial effects on the body. The optimal duration of the exercise period depends on the person's level of fitness and the type of exercise performed. Walking or jogging two to three miles, cycling or swimming for thirty minutes, or playing tennis for an hour or so will do the job if engaged in regularly at least every other day.

Physical fitness appears to have become a national craze, at least among young adults of the middle classes. But, in fact, the great majority of Americans still do not get enough exercise. For those who find exercise tedious or too time-consuming, the following pointers may be useful: First, you must get rid of the idea that exercise is undignified for a middle-aged man or woman. Second, do not equate exercise with sports, often deemed to be the province of the young. If you do not have the time or the inclination to engage in sports, you can still exercise. Third, exercise, like dieting, will not work if

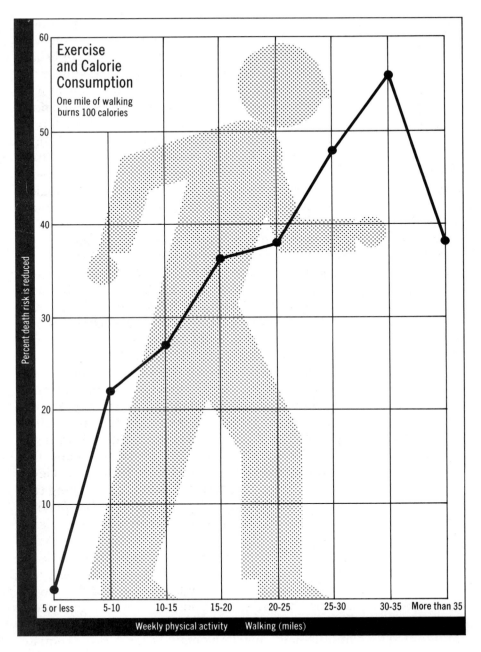

Exercise and Calorie Consumption

One mile of walking burns 100 calories

Percent death risk is reduced (y-axis): 10, 20, 30, 40, 50, 60

Weekly physical activity   Walking (miles)

5 or less | 5-10 | 10-15 | 15-20 | 20-25 | 25-30 | 30-35 | More than 35

FIGURE 2-4.

it is undertaken as a special crusade. In order for results to last, exercise must be incorporated into one's daily routine. It should at the least be painless, if not enjoyable. And, finally, it is better to do something—anything—than nothing. Even modest efforts can add up.[7] I find that riding a bike (10 minutes) or walking (30 minutes) to work and swimming (20 minutes) several days a week keeps me in fair shape.

Preventing Illness: Physical activity is closely linked to the prevention of illness. Over the last two decades there has been a significant decline in fatalities resulting from cardiovascular disease in the United States. This decrease has been attributed to changes in life-style (fewer smokers, lowering of blood cholesterol levels, greater physical fitness) as well as to better medical care (such as treatment for hypertension and care for coronary disease). To be part of this salutary trend, the middle-aged person should not only keep fit but should also maintain a calmly vigilant (but not anxious) watch over his or her body. The objective is to avoid undue damage and to detect early signs of illness. As you grow older, it becomes increasingly more important to conserve your body, because what breaks down gets harder to mend. There are some ailments that you cannot prevent, but you can take some other measures that will make a good deal of difference to your health.[8] The two most obvious avoidable health hazards are smoking and excessive drinking. If you have either of these problems, whatever it takes to stop you is well worth trying.

If you do not already have a personal physician, age fifty is the time to find one, and for you and he or she to get to know each other. The value of routine physical exams is debatable. Furthermore, medicine has a way of sometimes making patients out of normal people, so avoid unnecessary tests and procedures. But when there is a significant chance that something is wrong with you, don't postpone seeing a doctor, hoping for the best. On the other hand, a hypochondriacal preoccupation with your health will not make you live any longer—it will merely drain the joy out of your life.

3

SEXUALITY
AT
MIDLIFE

The past few decades have seen a marked change of attitude toward the role of sex during the older years. Until recently, it was assumed that there was little sexual interest among the elderly (except for a few "dirty" old men and women), and that of those who remained interested in sex, only a handful were able to manage it adequately. Now we are told that even those in advanced old age are sexually far more active than we imagined them to be. Furthermore, the perception of sex in the later years as a source of embarrassment has been replaced by a hearty endorsement of its merits. The image of an elderly couple dozing serenely side by side has been rehabilitated into one of tireless lovers copulating the night away. Once sex was supposed to die off with age; now it is said to get better with age.

Sexuality undergoes important changes with age, and these changes become apparent in the fifties if not earlier. It is important to understand what these changes are and to learn to deal with them. To what extent are alterations in sexual function physiologically based? Do these changes compromise sexual performance or merely lead to a somewhat different sexual experience? What is the role of psychological and social attitudes in dealing with these issues? This chapter will explore some of these questions.

SEXUAL ATTRACTION

Sexuality is important not only in and of itself but also because of its close association with our gender identity and our broader sense of selfhood or ego identity (the answer to "Who am I?"). The value placed on us by others, as well as our own self-esteem, is greatly influenced by how sexually desirable we are. Traditionally, physical attractiveness has been seen as a measure of the desirability of women as sexual partners, while social status has been considered more important for enhancing the sexual attractiveness of men. This discrepancy exists, in part, because sex is more intimately linked with considerations of dominance among males than among females.

Such factors are particularly important for understanding the sexual implications of changes in midlife. Think of it. Why should so many women be preoccupied with wrinkles and gray hair? What harm do they do? Why should men worry about their sagging chins, drooping shoulders, and expanding waistlines? The answer is that all of these changes signal to the world that we are getting old, and we fear that getting old means loss of sexual attractiveness and desire. That loss, in turn, means losing the vital spark of life and the loosening of the bonds of affection that bind us together.

It is easy enough to ascribe these attitudes to "ageism" and "sexism." But these are labels, not explanations; they beg the question. From an evolutionary perspective, we need to ask, Why is it that our bodies advertise the advent of old age? And why is it that the signs of aging have universally tended to detract from a person's sexual attractiveness rather than to enhance it?

The Evolutionary View: When viewed in evolutionary terms, humans and animals have two overriding incentives in life. One is to stay alive as long as possible, and the other is to produce as many offspring as possible. Through natural selection and/or sexual selection, some species and organisms prove to be more successful than others. From this perspective, the more you reproduce, the more "successful" you are in perpetuating your genes.[1] Males and females are both driven by this basic aim but they differ in the strategies by which they attain it.

Since man is capable of fathering countless children, while women are limited to a maximum of forty or so,[2] it would pay for males to be "promiscuous" and to go after "quantity," while women would be more selective and monogamous and would seek out "quality" in making sexual choices. Men would be aroused more by the physical characteristics of women, while women would look for additional attributes that would make men reliable and effective mates. In purely reproductive terms, the postmenopausal woman would be a reproductive dead-end and therefore less attractive to men bent on fertilization. Older males, because they remain reproductively capable, would lose their sexual charms more slowly, and their social status would compensate for their loss of sexual fitness.

In the modern world, the prospect of living as long as possible still resonates with our deeply held hopes. But the urge to have as many children as possible makes no sense. Yet long-established behavioral patterns presumably still motivate us to behave in ways that are neither rational nor fully conscious. That they may not make sense in today's modern world does not in itself prevent us from following the dictates of the distant past. The fundamental motivation that drives us to act sexually remains reproductive in intent even though we may simultaneously do everything humanly possible to prevent that consequence through birth control. It therefore follows that the more obvious the reproductive capacity of the potential sexual partner, the more sexually arousing that person continues to be. This makes age a liability, and more so for women than for men, unless we actively counteract the force of motivational factors rooted in our evolutionary heritage that are no longer adaptive in the world of today. We no longer live in the trees and we need not go on behaving as though we do.

This discrepancy between the two sexes is further compounded by the fact that men are consequently in socially more dominant positions, and their power and prestige usually increases with age for at least a decade or so beyond midlife. This is why older men in positions of power tend to retain more of their sexual appeal than women of comparable age.

Men typically choose younger mates, whereas women are rarely afforded the same privilege—if that is indeed a privilege. And there are many more polygamous societies than polyandrous ones. These sex discrepancies have been most marked in cultures where men have wielded autocratic power. Yet, in subtle forms, the same tendencies are still very much in evidence. A fifty-year-old man seen in the company of a twenty-five-year-old wife or lover generates a very different kind of social reaction than a fifty-year-old woman with a twenty-five-year-old husband or lover. If sexual interactions are seen in the light of this rather ruthless process, age inevitably loses to youth, with men hanging in there longer than women.

The Changing Perspective: These traditional patterns are now changing, with some women dating, and occasionally marrying, younger men, but the shift to parity in this respect is still far from being complete. In the modern world, reproduction is no longer primary, and women are no longer secondary. The very perception of what constitutes sexual attractiveness is undergoing considerable change, and women are becoming far more autonomous in the conduct of their sexual lives.

A great deal more ground must be covered in both areas, however, if significant changes are to take place in our sexual proclivities and patterns of behavior. Our standards of physical and sexual attractiveness are still inexorably youth-oriented. Think of the advertisements for perfumes, lingerie, bathing suits—anything that entails a measure of nudity and eroticism. As a rule, the models are young or youthful-looking women. The implication is that to be sexy you must be young. And if you are not young, then you should try to look young. So we have a multibillion-dollar cosmetic industry to help us fake youth.

Physical appearance in midlife is largely determined by heredity and the level of health and fitness one maintains. The first is not completely under your control, but there is a great deal that you can do with respect to the second. Unfortunately, it is harder to eat right and to keep physically active than to lie back in a beautician's chair and let someone else do the work. Cosmetics and clothing have their place, but they cannot be the mainstay of retaining our sexual appeal. And as we grow older, our personality, rather than our looks, will have to be our main asset.

We are pressed to emulate not only the appearance of youth, but its erotic demeanor as well. Sex for the young is fast and furious. It is ignited easily and fizzles out like fireworks. It is turned on by appearances and tends to stay skin deep. Some of us grow old but never outgrow this style. Hence, as we age we find ourselves and our partners increasingly less satisfactory.

Others develop a deeper eroticism with the passage of years. Looks continue to matter but only as the appetizer. The sensual quality of the person, rather than the body as such, becomes the main course. While time ravages the surface of the skin, it gives polish and patina to the self. By looking after your body instead of merely painting over its blemishes, you continue to project the sense of vitality that is the true essence of sexual attraction.

For only a minority of women do sexual relations become less important with the menopause, and that decrease may have as much to do with their partners as with themselves. The whole notion of "change of life" conveys a false picture: Women do not undergo fundamental personality changes simply because they stop menstruating. Midlife women—like everyone else—have many concerns, but it is an error to attribute those concerns to the menopause solely because they happen to coincide with it. Getting older, losing husbands, developing cancer—these and related worries weigh more heavily on the middle-aged woman's mind than the menopause.

SEXUAL DRIVE

We are propelled into sexual activity in response to erotic sights, sounds, smells, and tactile stimulation, as well as through erotic fantasies. Although precious little research has been done in this area, there is no reason to suspect that the relative importance of these sensory modalities changes in middle age.

The one significant exception is that the power of psychologically erotic stimuli declines with age among males, whereas that of physical stimulation remains unabated. Teenage boys will respond erotically to a very wide variety of erotic cues. Virtually any sort of emotional arousal may elicit an erection (in one case reported by Kinsey, listening to the national anthem brought on this effect). In one's excitable youth, emotional and erotic arousal overlap. With increasing age this tendency mercifully subsides so that by adulthood only psychological stimuli of a frankly erotic nature will normally induce sexual arousal.

In midlife, purely psychological stimuli become less capable of eliciting sexual excitement, although physical stimulation is still effective. Middle-aged couples may be misled into thinking that this change heralds a sexual decline as an accompaniment to aging. It is not hard to imagine the reaction of a menopausal woman when she realizes that the sight of her nudity is no longer as arousing to her husband as it was in earlier times. While the change in her appearance may not be irrelevant, the shift in the response pattern of the husband is equally important. Greater reliance on physical stimulation helps to keep the sexual life of such a couple alive, but a sense of resignation condemns it to gradual decline.

Every sexual response is a reaction to some stimulus, be it external or internal; these stimuli in themselves are powerless to affect us if the capacity and readiness to respond are absent. Furthermore, we do not passively wait to be sexually aroused but actively seek stimuli that will arouse us. This motivational force and capacity to respond sexually is what we mean by the "sexual drive" (what Freud called the *libido*).

The Role of Hormones: There is no general agreement about the nature of the sexual drive; such "instinctual" forces are thought to be innate, although greatly modified by learning. It is a fair bet that the sexual drive is at some level generated and sustained by hormones, and present evidence points to testosterone as the substance that patterns the brain (the "organizational effect") and maintains the sex drive (the "activational effect") in both sexes. But it would be misleading to think of testosterone or any other hormone as some sort of "sex fuel" that drives our sexual engines.

Like other biological factors, hormones provide a necessary but insufficient basis for sexual behavior. Among animals the effects of sex hormones are much more compelling; among humans they are greatly modified by psychological variables. While hormonal deficiencies interfere with erotic desire and sexual functions, hormonal normality by no means ensures sexual vitality.

The relationship of hormones and sexuality is particularly important in puberty and midlife. The activation of the hypothalamic-pituitary-gonadal system may be the basis of the upsurge of adolescent sexuality, and the decline in hormonal function may be linked to the reduced frequency of sexual activity that accompanies aging. But that linkage makes more sense for men than for women. This statement may sound paradoxical in light of the fact that the dramatic reduction in hormone output occurs in women, not men. But the hormones we are concerned with are the androgens (mainly testosterone)—and not the estrogens and progestins that drop so sharply during the menopause—because androgens appear to be the hormones that are primarily linked to the sexual drive.

Frequency of Coitus: The frequency of sexual activity generally decreases with age for both sexes, although there are, of course, exceptions. However, this decrease does not start at age fifty. When the wife is younger than thirty, the frequency of coitus drops by 25 percent during the first four years of marriage. Among males in the Kinsey study, the frequency of orgasm per week (from all sexual activities combined) began to drop at about age thirty (from a mean of three and a median of two per week). For women a similar decline sets in at about age forty (from a mean of close to two and a median of one per week). Other studies that have focused on the frequency of sexual intercourse have consistently shown similar decreases.[3]

In trying to explain this pattern, investigators have focused on the female and the male separately, as well as on their relationships. Kinsey claimed that the reduced frequency of sexual activity in the middle and later years was due to the waning interest and potency of the male. Menopausal and older women remained sexually interested but had increasing difficulty in finding active and able sexual partners. Some women actually showed an upsurge in sexual interest, explained on physiological grounds by the fact that androgen production during the menopause does not lessen, and its erotogenic effect is now unopposed by the dampening effect of estrogen and progesterone. It is a bit like taking your foot off the brake without stepping on the accelerator.

Also important are psychological factors such as freedom from the fear of pregnancy for postmenopausal women, the greater assertiveness manifested by women in midlife, and the opportunity to attend to their own personal needs after years of looking after the needs of their children.

While this more optimistic image is now the dominant view, there is no reliable data to show that the claim of enhanced sexual interest and activity can be extended to a substantial proportion of women at midlife. Other evidence indicates that sexual interest among middle-aged women actually shows a distinct drop.

In the male, explanations based on reduced hormonal levels are not conclusive. Testosterone slowly lessens with age but generally does not dip to a subnormal level. Only when there is a definite deficiency of male hormones are sexual functions disrupted; most middle-aged and older men have no such deficiency. Furthermore, the reduction in sexual activity precedes the decline in testosterone level.[4]

Sex is vulnerable to a variety of disturbances of the vascular, endocrine, nervous, and other systems of the body. But disturbances in these systems are a result of ill health, not of aging as such. Sexual activity is sometimes burdened and disrupted by psychological and interpersonal causes, and of these middle age has its share. Anxiety and depression, from whatever cause, play havoc with sexual interest and performance. Career disappointments, financial worries, loss of status and self-esteem, and the drudgery of everyday life all take their toll. The departure of their children confronts a couple with the prospect of a life together all by themselves. This may be the occasion for sexual rediscovery and freedom, but in an unhappy marriage it is not a cheerful prospect.

Women are particularly vulnerable to the loss of a stable sexual partner, typically a husband. Ill health or anything else that interferes with a husband's sexual interest and ability may seriously compromise a wife's sexual life as well, since relatively few women in this age group seek extramarital sexual relationships (although this tendency is becoming somewhat more widespread).

The interpersonal context of sexual relationships is important for both sexes but, because of psychological and social factors, influences the behavior of women more significantly. Women are no less interested in sex than men, but they feel more secure and fulfilled if sex takes place within the context of a meaningful and stable relationship. Not only is this their preference, but were they to behave differently, as men are more inclined to, they would be more harshly judged by society. Men also feel more secure and fulfilled in a stable relationship, but they are more willing to engage in sex outside of such relationships as well.

As a result, marriage has been the single most significant factor in shaping a woman's sexual behavior. Although this generalization may apply less to the present generation of younger women, it remains largely true for women in midlife and older. Loss of a spouse through death or divorce and the problem of finding a satisfactory replacement in middle age does not mean that women inevitably become resigned to a sexually barren existence. Among fifty-year-old women who have been married before, 37 percent continue to engage in sexual inter-course (the figure goes down to 12 percent by age sixty).[5] At fifty-five, the frequency of coitus among these women is only two-thirds that of married women of the same age but double that of sexually active women who have never married.

Researchers have reported significant differences in the behavior of divorced and widowed women: The divorced are twice as likely to engage in coitus as the widowed (82 percent compared to 43 percent), but beyond age fifty this difference narrows. Although divorce and widowhood both entail the loss of a marital partner, they are quali-tatively different with respect to what antedates and what follows the end of the marriage. A third of divorced women, for example, report having had affairs while married, compared to less than a tenth of the widowed. Because there is a greater attachment to the lost hus-band on the part of the widowed, fewer widows (27 percent) than divorcees (47 percent) remarry.

OTHER SEXUAL BEHAVIORS

Coitus is the primary but not the only sexual outlet for the middle-aged. Sexual fantasy and masturbation remain very common in midlife, and a minority of men and women engage in homosexual relationships.

Masturbation: Public attitudes toward masturbation have mellowed considerably in recent years, but the practice is still viewed in mildly negative terms by many. Although no one need worry about the health consequences of masturbation (which are nonexistent), there is considerable embarrassment (even on the part of teenagers) in admitting to the practice, as it may suggest that one is not "good enough" to attract a sexual partner. Sex therapists and other workers in the field, on the other hand, heartily endorse the practice whenever there is the need or the inclination for it.

Because men are more genitally focused, they are more likely than women to have recourse to masturbation. But a substantial proportion of women also rely on masturbation, especially when they have no access to a sexual partner: At age fifty the prevalence of masturbation among the previously married is twice that for married women. In purely physical terms, there is no consistent difference between orgasm attained through masturbation or through coitus.

Homosexual Relations: Homosexuality has come out of the closet over the last two decades, yet we still do not know very much about it. Estimates of its prevalence vary, but exclusively homosexual individuals probably constitute less than 5 percent of the general population.

Although their sexual orientation is established long before, some homosexuals do not come out of the closet until midlife. These are usually bisexual married men whose children are grown. Their marriages may break up as a result, or a compromise may be worked out if there are enough other incentives for them and their wives to stay together.

Those who have been in long-term gay partnerships face more or less the same issues of sexuality in midlife as their heterosexual counterparts. But those who have been playing the field (more true for gay men than women) now face a difficult period, because the effect of age is even more damaging to the sexual appeal of male homosexuals than heterosexuals. At least in the past, many older gay men have had to seek young male prostitutes as sexual partners.

The similarities between homosexual and heterosexual relationships are far greater than their differences. The one basic distinction is, of course, that exclusively gay men and women have no children. But in this respect, they are basically no different from childless heterosexual couples.

ALTERATIONS IN SEXUAL RESPONSE

Whatever the poetry and romance of sex and whatever the moral and social significance of human sexual behavior," wrote Alfred Kinsey, "sexual responses involve real and material changes in the physiological functioning of an animal."[6] Understanding these alterations in the physiology of the sexual response at midlife requires some background in the general nature of the sexual response cycle.

In response to effective sexual stimulation (physical or psychological), the first phase of the sexual response cycle is erotic arousal or

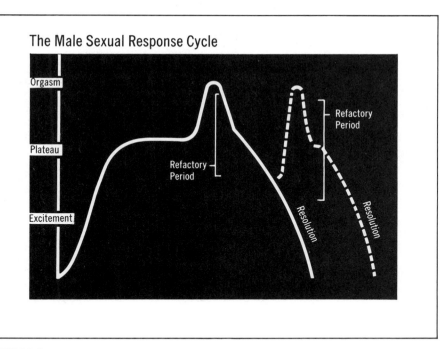

The Male Sexual Response Cycle

Orgasm

Plateau

Refactory
Period

Refactory
Period

Excitement

Resolution

Resolution

FIGURE 3-1.

excitement (see Figures 3-1 and 3-2). The *plateau phase,* a period of sustained arousal, follows. If effective sexual stimulation is continued it leads to *orgasm,* followed by the fourth and last phase, *resolution,* during which organs and tissues return to their resting condition.[7]

This pattern generally holds true for both sexes except for a few differences. In the male, following orgasm there is a "refractory period" during which the body is unable to respond to further stimulation until an obligatory period of rest has elapsed. This refractory period may last anywhere from a few minutes to several hours. Women generally do not have such a refractory period, so with effective stimulation they may have consecutive (or "multiple") orgasms in short order.

Although the responses to sexual arousal and orgasm are focused in the genital region, they are by no means restricted to it. Reactions in the rest of the body also accompany this process. For example, the nipples become erect in response to sexual excitement and the breasts swell. The skin shows flushing, temperature changes, and perspiration. The heart rate accelerates as does the pace and depth of breathing. In short, it is the body as a whole, rather than the genital organs

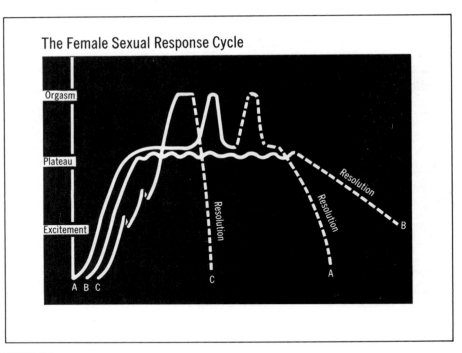

The Female Sexual Response Cycle

Orgasm

Plateau

Excitement

A B C

Resolution

Resolution

Resolution

C

A

B

FIGURE 3-2.

in isolation, that reacts to sexual arousal and goes through the manifestations of orgasm.

All of the changes manifested by the body can be explained on the basis of two physiological mechanisms. One is *vasocongestion*, which consists of the engorgement of blood vessels and tissues that results when more blood rushes in than can be drained away. The prime example of vasocongestion in the male is erection of the penis. The penis becomes stiff just as a garden hose becomes stiff when the water is turned on. In the female, the swelling of the clitoris, the major and minor lips of the vulva, the outer third of the vagina, and the breasts is the outcome of the same process.

The second mechanism is increased muscular tension, or *myotonia*. As blood rushes into the tissues during the excitement phase, muscular tension gradually builds up in the muscles of the pelvic region and elsewhere in the body, culminating in the rhythmic contractions characteristic of orgasm in both sexes. Once this neuromuscular tension has been released through orgasm, myotonia and vasocongestion recede simultaneously during the resolution phase (see Figures 3-3 and 3-4).

These physiological processes are controlled by intricate neurophysiological mechanisms located in the spinal cord and the brain. The autonomic portion of the spinal cord has centers that control erection and ejaculation at a reflexive level and can operate independently of higher centers. But ordinarily it is the brain centers that control all sexual functions and are interconnected with the complex processes dealing with thoughts and emotions. A twinge of anxiety over sex may sabotage the smooth functioning of the sexual response cycle in a man or woman who is otherwise sexually healthy.

During midlife the changes that take place in the workings of this system are comparable to those of the heart, the lungs, and other parts of the body. The capacity to respond to sexual stimulation and attain orgasm remains viable as long as one is alive. The four-phase sexual response cycle keeps its sequence unaltered, although some slow but definite changes modify the various aspects of this sexual response cycle.

Our knowledge of sexual physiology is still in its infancy. We are therefore far from clear about the details of how and when the changes in the sexual response cycle come about during the adult years. As with any physiological process, researchers encounter a great deal of variability among individuals. When we discuss the changes in sexual response associated with aging, we are inevitably talking about some hypothetical average that artificially levels everyone into a common pattern. In reality, individuals may deviate from this pattern so widely that some fifty-year-old men and women respond more like forty-year-olds and others like sixty-year-olds. Changes usually start in the fifties, but for some the onset is earlier, for others later. Though most fifty-year-olds are likely to show some of the effects of aging on sexual function, these effects are not prominent until the older years. In that sense, the pattern is no different from the wrinkling of the skin.

The general rule applicable to both sexes is that with aging there is a gradual attenuation in the intensity of the manifestations of the sexual response cycle. The older male's sexual response to erotic stimulation is slower; for example, the older a man gets the more time he needs to achieve erection, no matter how exciting the stimulation.

Erections tend to be softer and the angle of the erect penis is less acute (that is, the penis points less upward). The clear fluid that appears in droplets at the top of the penis (the secretions from the Cowper's glands) is scantier. Once erection has been achieved, the older male cannot maintain an erection as long as a younger one can. The older male who is sexually more experienced and self-confident,

Changes in Male Sex Organs During the Sexual Response Cycle

EXCITEMENT PHASE

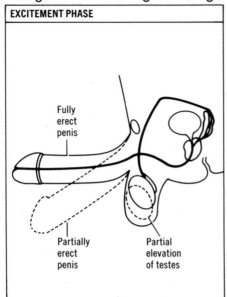

Fully erect penis

Partially erect penis

Partial elevation of testes

PLATEAU PHASE

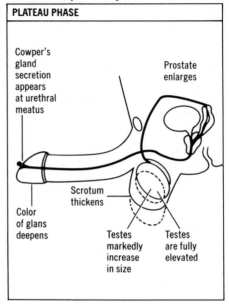

Cowper's gland secretion appears at urethral meatus

Prostate enlarges

Scrotum thickens

Color of glans deepens

Testes markedly increase in size

Testes are fully elevated

ORGASMIC PHASE

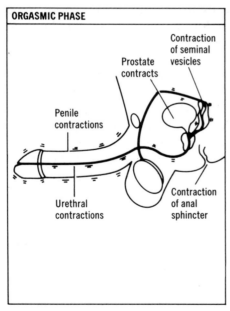

Prostate contracts

Contraction of seminal vesicles

Penile contractions

Urethral contractions

Contraction of anal sphincter

RESOLUTION PHASE

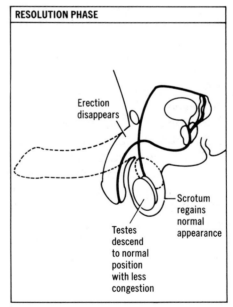

Erection disappears

Testes descend to normal position with less congestion

Scrotum regains normal appearance

FIGURE 3-3.

Changes in Female Sex Organs During the Sexual Response Cycle

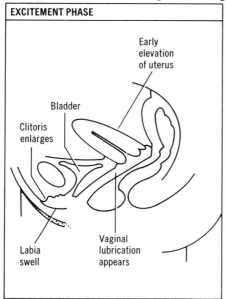

EXCITEMENT PHASE

Early elevation of uterus

Bladder

Clitoris enlarges

Labia swell

Vaginal lubrication appears

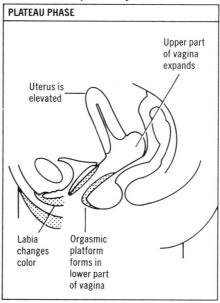

PLATEAU PHASE

Upper part of vagina expands

Uterus is elevated

Labia changes color

Orgasmic platform forms in lower part of vagina

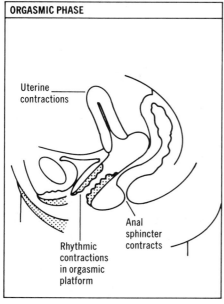

ORGASMIC PHASE

Uterine contractions

Rhythmic contractions in orgasmic platform

Anal sphincter contracts

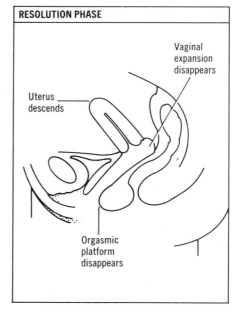

RESOLUTION PHASE

Vaginal expansion disappears

Uterus descends

Orgasmic platform disappears

FIGURE 3-4.

however, is much less likely to ejaculate prematurely than the younger male. Having overcome the anxiety and hair-trigger response of the younger years, and before succumbing to the waning of virility of the older years, a man may have more lasting power in middle age than at any other time in his life. But if the older male loses his erection before orgasm, he will encounter greater difficulty in reviving it. Similarly, once orgasm has been reached, the older a man gets, the more time he will need and the more difficulty he will experience in attaining a subsequent orgasm during a given period of lovemaking; in other words, the refractory period gets longer with age.

The male's orgasmic reactions also become less intense with age. Contractions are fewer, ejaculation is less vigorous, and the volume of the ejaculate is smaller. While the intensity of the physiological responses clearly diminishes over time, however, the subjective experience of orgasm continues to be highly satisfying, though not as explosive in nature as it was in previous years. Finally, during the resolution phase the effects of vasocongestion and increased muscular tension revert with greater speed. Whereas penile detumescence is a gradual process in the younger male, it becomes progressively more abrupt as a man gets older.

As a result of the menopause, a woman undergoes significant changes in the structure of her reproductive system: The vaginal walls become thinner and paler and lose their corrugated texture and elasticity. Vaginal lubrication during sexual arousal occurs more slowly and is less profuse. The orgasmic platform develops less fully and the extent of vasocongestion in the labial folds is also less marked. During the orgasmic and resolution phases, the vagina of the older woman behaves very much like the penis of the older male: Orgasmic contractions are fewer and less intense, and resolution occurs more promptly.

These changes are not abnormalities and do not preclude the enjoyment of sex in midlife and later years. But they may cause problems for some individuals. The thinning of the vaginal walls and the diminution of the lubricatory response, for instance, may make sexual intercourse painful or cause irritation of the urinary bladder. These problems, which usually become manifest later than age fifty, can be prevented by estrogen replacement therapy, or relieved by the application of an appropriate lubricant. Most importantly, the more sexually active a woman is, the less the likelihood that these changes will become troublesome. There seems to be a close association between diminishing frequency of intercourse and the lowering of estrogen levels even though the mechanism underlying this process is unclear.

Because sexual functions are affected by age, their sustenance and satisfaction require that we be realistic in our sexual expectations. The greater vulnerability of sexual function at this time necessitates that we also consider the problem of sexual dysfunction.

SEXUAL DYSFUNCTION

Sexual disturbances are not as discrete entities as are the disorders of other bodily systems and are much more affected by subjective perceptions. Furthermore, sexual dysfunctions must be differentiated from other disturbances of the reproductive system (such as sterility), gender disorders (such as transsexualism), and variations in sexual behaviors and orientation (such as voyeurism or sadomasochism).

Types of Genital Dysfunction: Sexual dysfunction refers specifically to disorders in sexual desire, performance, or satisfaction. One of the most common forms of sexual dysfunction is the inhibition of sexual desire, manifested by a persistent and pervasive lack of sexual interest. Disturbances of sexual excitement may result in problems with erections in males (impotence) and vaginal lubricatory responses in females. Disturbances of orgasm in the male typically take the form of premature ejaculation and sometimes of failure to ejaculate. The female may experience undue delay or inability to reach orgasm despite the attainment of normal sexual arousal. Painful sexual intercourse (dyspareunia) is a rare problem for men but a more common one for women. It is typically caused by spasm of the musculature surrounding the vaginal opening, which may be due to psychological factors or to various forms of pelvic pathology. With this problem a woman may be able to engage in sexual intercourse only at the cost of considerable discomfort. In extreme cases the spasm of the vaginal opening (vaginismus) is severe enough to make intromission impossible. A variety of physical, intrapsychic, or interpersonal problems and conflicts may be responsible for causing such conditions. Usually multiple factors are involved.

Causes of Sexual Dysfunction: Sexual dysfunction during midlife may be viewed from three different perspectives. First, the normal physiological changes that occur in midlife are misperceived as evidence of sexual failure. For instance, when a man in his fifties has a somewhat softer erection, which takes longer to achieve and is more liable to be lost before orgasm, he may leap to the erroneous conclusion that he is becoming impotent. Similarly, a menopausal woman with reduced vaginal lubrication in response to sexual arousal may find intercourse uncomfortable and therefore conclude that sex can no longer be pleasurable.

Second, sexual dysfunction can result from physical illness. While this may occur at any age, the older one gets the greater is the likelihood of illness interfering with sexual function. Virtually any serious systemic disease or pelvic pathology may result in the disruption of sexual mechanisms. Disturbances of the circulatory, endocrine, and nervous systems are more likely to cause problems, especially when their effects are combined, as in advanced diabetes. The medications that influence these systems (such as certain antihypertensive drugs) are often as much at fault as are certain other drugs or alcohol.[8] Some forms of prostatic surgery may also be particularly damaging to sexual function.

Third, since sexual intercourse entails an interaction between two individuals, sexual dysfunction often reflects disturbances in the couple's relationship, which may or may not be related to sexual issues as such. Power struggles, or the degree to which one's dependency needs are being satisfied, for example, may spill over into the sexual realm. Sex, one of the basic currencies of interpersonal exchange, is likely to be contaminated by any difficulties that exist in other aspects of a couple's relationship; conversely, sexual problems are likely to intrude into the nonsexual realms of life. The sexual problems of this time of life are therefore often more general problems superimposed on the sexual realm. The increased vulnerability of sexual functions then compounds the problem into a sexual dysfunction.

Because so much attention has been focused on the menopause and the effects of aging on women, one may be led to believe that female rather than male sexuality is more likely to be disrupted at midlife. The contrary is true.[9] A decrease in sexual desire as reflected in sexual fantasy and activity shows up more markedly in men than in women. This may be due to age-related reduction in testosterone levels or may be associated with the stress and depression of the midlife transition to which men and the male sex drive are more vulnerable. Another reason why difficulties in sexual performance are more likely to afflict men than women in midlife is that men suffer more ill health than women, and their use of drugs and alcohol is more apt to lead to sexual disturbances.

Under most circumstances, sexual intercourse places a greater burden of performance on a man. Though couples share a dual responsibility to provide pleasure to each other and to the self, the failure of the man to get an erection is more disruptive to coitus, in purely mechanical form, than is a woman's failure to reach orgasm. This disparity is compounded by the traditional expectation that the man should take the initiative and manage the sexual act to mutual satisfaction. By placing the woman in the position of the instrument and casting himself as the virtuoso, he takes the primary responsibility for the quality of the music.

A particular problem for the midlife male is that the physiological changes that normally take place in the sexual response cycle threaten the very function on which so much of his self-esteem has come to depend. Especially vulnerable are men who are highly performance-oriented, competitive, and independent.

The personality changes that men and women undergo at midlife may mitigate or compound these difficulties. Women tend to become more independent and self-assertive, while men become more dependent and less assertive in their intimate relationships with women. When all goes well, these shifts in personality make men and women more alike and help to draw them together, creating a chance for greater commitment and intimacy than ever before. In this affectionate and secure setting, couples have no difficulty adapting their sexual activities to the physiological changes of their bodies. They may make love less often but under more optimal circumstances. They make greater allowances for each other and achieve a manner of lovemaking more artfully suited to each other's needs.

The potential for trouble is ever present, however, for those whose relationship has all along left much to be desired: The pigeons now come home to roost after years of neglect and suppressed anger. Or a marginally satisfactory relationship may now succumb to the simultaneous demands for adjustment on the physical and psychological fronts. When this happens, sex is usually the first casualty.

For some men, increased dependence on their wives in midlife revives unresolved childhood conflicts. A husband who has dominated his wife for years may begin to act toward her like an anxious and clinging child. Women generally do not find being clung to any more romantic or sexually arousing than being pushed around. A man may carry the transformation of wife into mother to the point where, although he continues to respect and love her, he is no longer sexually aroused by her. He then becomes particularly tempted to seek his sexual satisfaction with other women.

Women who have been patronized, neglected, and abused by men for years gain the opportunity to retaliate at midlife. In cases where the woman's rebellion leads to male sexual dysfunction, sexual sabotage is the most commonly used device. Sometimes a woman will outrightly refuse to sleep with her husband any more, alleging reasons of health, coital discomfort, lack of sexual desire, or some other face-saving pretext. She may, however, accomplish the same purpose without announcing her intention. If her husband has routinely mounted and dismounted her after a few perfunctory caresses, she can let him go right ahead with business as usual. Except that as yesterday's pliant wife turns into an inert body, he fails to become aroused anymore.

A man is more dependent in midlife than in his earlier years on elaborate sexual fantasies, varied forms of erotic stimulation, and a caring and skillful sexual partner. Couples who have together steadily grown sexually more sophisticated over the years have nothing to fear. But clumsiness compounded over the years cannot be overcome on demand at midlife. If a wife has served her husband's sexual needs out of a sense of duty, and with little pleasure for herself, she will see no justification for her meeting his more varied and onerous sexual requirements at a time when she is looking forward to being relieved of all sexual obligations.

Ironically, oversolicitousness may do as much harm as indifference. A wife who anxiously hovers over the struggles of a limp penis is not likely to enhance the chances of a favorable outcome. The last thing a man wants is to be treated like a sexual invalid.

Women who have led active and satisfying sexual lives are less likely than men to suffer sexual dysfunction in midlife. Only in a minority of cases (perhaps one in ten) does the menopause, as such, appear to lead to a diminution of sexual desire and a loss of sexual responsiveness.

Women, like men, may suffer from the consequences of physical ailments. But more often than not a woman's sexual life is handicapped mainly because of the problems of her husband, the disruption of her marriage or other intimate relationship, and the lack of a sexual partner of her liking.

SEXUAL MAINTENANCE

The first requisite for the care and maintenance of sexuality in midlife is a healthy and vigorous body. Although an active sex life is possible even in the presence of considerable chronic illness, sexual desire often succumbs to poor health. No less important is the care and renewal of our intimate relationships with our sexual partners. Even though physiological factors become increasingly important as we grow older, in the final analysis the human ties are the key determinants of the quality of our sexual lives.

Hormone Replacement: Since the symptoms of the menopause are due to the sharp decline of ovarian estrogens, the logical remedy would be to replace these hormones. Current medical consensus is that estrogen replacement is valuable for women when there are no contraindications to its use. Such treatment, however, must use the lowest effective doses of hormones for the shortest possible period of time, and must be carried out under medical supervision. Because estrogens are potent drugs, the decision must be based on a cost-benefit assessment in each individual case, reached in collaboration between doctor and patient.

Estrogens are usually taken orally as pills but may also be used locally as vaginal creams, which are absorbed into the bloodstream. In the absence of such therapy, and if necessary in addition to it, the use of lubricants (which should be water-based like K-Y Jelly, rather than oil-based like Vaseline) takes care of the problem of vaginal dryness during coitus.

Unless a man has low testosterone levels, and only a few do, he does not need hormonal replacement. Nor is there any good evidence that the various exotic extracts and potions that are supposed to be sexually rejuvenating are effective.

Sexual Activity: If you want to stay sexually alive, you must keep sexually active. Men and women who remain sexually active are more likely to retain their sexual vigor and interest into their older years—another illustration of the adage, "Use it or lose it." This advice calls for a deliberate effort on the part of couples to create opportunities for making love—as long as it does not become one more duty to discharge.

If practical and moral considerations preclude playing the field in temporary liaisons, autoeroticism offers not only a means of sexual release, but also a source of erotic satisfaction as an end in itself. You may be taken aback by the suggestion that masturbation is sometimes the answer to sexual frustration. If so, you can look at it as a means of keeping sexually active so that when you do link up with a partner of your choice, the machinery will be in good working order.

The Need for Adaptation: As with other bodily and psychological functions, sex requires a number of adjustments and adaptations in midlife. For those who are reasonably healthy and blessed with caring and compatible partners, these shifts are not hard to make.

Without the pressure to perform, a midlife couple can figure out when, where, and under what circumstances coitus seems to work best. They may make love less often and at times that allow the most leisure. Rather than delaying it to the eleventh hour at night, they may engage in sex on weekend afternoons or in the mornings. They make greater allowances for each other, and their lovemaking is more artfully suited to the needs of each.

Sustaining Intimacy: Sexual partners who have been together for a long time have the benefits of trust and affection. In the younger years of marriage, sex tends to be a battleground where scores are settled and peace is made, but if a couple has stuck together until middle age, sex should become a demilitarized zone. The problem they now face is the numbing effect of habituation. For habit, to paraphrase Balzac, is the monster that devours marital sex.

In some relationships, the wife comes to accept sex as an extension of her marital responsibilities—one more way to keep her husband happy—but there is no romance to it. The husband, in turn, may view marital sex like home cooking: It is wholesome and nutritious, and as long as he is paying for it, he might just as well enjoy it, even though there is no spice to it.

The introduction of a new sexual partner into the picture will add more spice. Moral considerations aside, one could make a case for extramarital relationships in a variety of forms. Some husbands and wives operate on the principle that what you don't know can't hurt you. Others will not put up with secrecy or deception in any form, but are willing to allow the spouse to have other lovers as long as the option is open to both partners and the marital relationship retains its primacy. Those who explore the wilder shores of love experiment with triads, spousal exchanges, group sex, or any number of other permutations. But "reason" rarely prevails over the dictates of the heart in these arrangements. The stakes are even higher when the extramarital partners are younger than the midlife couple.

Much has been made in the past decade of the merits of "open" marriages. But it may be that, as Francine du Plessix Gray has put it, "both the discipline of fidelity and a measured use of the untruth offer more alternatives for the future than the brutal sincerity of open marriages."[10]

If you have given up on your marriage, an affair is as good a way to end it as any, and more fun than most. But if you want to keep your spouse, you are clearly risking your marriage. On the other hand, transient affairs, carried out with discretion, are known to tide some men and women over difficult periods of their marital relationships.

In midlife many people do not have willing and able sexual partners, a problem that faces more women than men, and one that grows with advancing age. The "swinging singles" life-style does not really appeal to many mature women, and eligible men who are interested in long-term relationships are more likely to look for younger women. Many unattached women could get married if they lowered their standards, but they do not choose to do so. There is no easy solution to this issue, to which we shall return again in discussing kith and kin in midlife.

More Out of Less: In purely physical terms, the effect of age on sex is not different from its impact on other aspects of life. But with respect to other physical functions, we gain nothing by growing older. It is different with sex. With the passage of time, it is possible to expand sex into a different and in some ways a richer experience, which amply compensates for whatever deficits are incurred through changes in the sexual response cycle.

The sexual machinery of the young is like a vehicle with four-wheel drive. It can cover any terrain, but it gives you a bumpy ride. Sex in the younger years tends to be more anxious. There is the fear as well as the failure of pregnancy. Sex is bait and battleground. Each performance must eclipse all others, be it one's own or those of real or imaginary rivals.

To be an accomplished lover in midlife requires a change in styles and standards. By the time a man attains fifty, the sexual trials and tribulations of youth must be left behind. Over the years, his sexual credit and credibility have been long established. So what if his penis does not snap to attention or point to the ceiling as it used to? Failure to have an erection need not be mortifying to a man with the right attitude. Erections come and go—so what else is new? The middle-aged man has a better chance to break away from his genital fixation, to become the master rather than the servant of his sexual organ. Maturity will make him more like a woman and hence a better lover. If this sounds paradoxical, it is because we have accepted a false dichotomy between masculinity and femininity whereby they are seen as antithetical to each other.

OLD KNOTS JUST GET STRONGER*
by Jon Carroll

There is something perfect and easy about the embrace of a longtime lover. The arms slip easily through; left up, right down, whatever; the decisions have been made although not announced.

Noses and chins and foreheads and optical appliances sort themselves out without struggle or strain; planning is not required. You mesh like well-designed gears; you fold into each other like melted butter and sweet cream; you slide like otters through calm waters.

You kiss before you know that you are kissing. The impulse; the act; nothing between.

It is said that people who have been together for a long time begin to resemble one another. It is equally possible to believe that familiarity has bred natural bumps and hollows in the body. A concave spot in the shoulder, a certain crook of the elbow, a knee automatically bent to preserve equilibrium.

Made for each other.

Literally.

This is a song about Valentine's Day, but it is not a song about young love. The confusion about young love is immediate and complete; the confusion of old love is complete and eternal. The first mystery has been solved; it is the mystery beyond (more complex, more amusing, more satisfying) that rivets the attention now.

These are embarrassing matters. New love is not embarrassing, at least not to the new lovers. So heavily involved are they in private embarrassment—I didn't mean, I never thought, of course you, certainly you, a thousand times

A similar transformation is required of a woman. When she no longer needs to search for a father for her children, she can choose the man for herself. The reticence, coyness, and bargaining that by choice or by necessity tend to characterize female sexual behavior in younger years can now be abandoned in favor of a more open, bolder,

you—that public embarrassment fades into the wallpaper.

But eventually we swim up to consciousness again, and we become more circumspect. Compared to the volumes written about the first flush of passion, the words composed about longtime love would fill no more than a slim book.

A slim book with wide margins.

A slim book that soon finds its way to the bargain bins.

Affection informed by tolerance and patience is not a commercial emotion. Old friends and old lovers are valued privately, which is probably as it should be.

We get along; we go along; the ecstasy is implicit. Implicit ecstasy would seem to be paradox; the continuing experience, however, denies the apparent contradiction.

Then there is this moment in the longtime love affair: the moment of intellectual joy.

You have seen this person in every conceivable context. You have seen her (or him; you may freely substitute "or him") at her absolute worst. Also at her best. Also during the boring moments in between.

You have seen her sleeping, unaware, innocent, slack-mouthed. You have seen her awake, interested, bolt-upright, unself-conscious, eyes glittering, gathering information. You have seen her awkward and graceful; you have seen her reaping and sowing.

And just when you think you have discovered all the somethings about her, there is something else. Valentine's Day would be a stupid holiday, were it not for that.

Were it not for the unknown at the center of the known.

Were it not for the pulse of the blood under your hands.

Were it not for the embrace of the longtime lover.

* Published in the *San Francisco Chronicle* February 14, 1986. Copyright *San Francisco Chronicle*, 1986. Reprinted by permission.

and freer giving of herself. This makes a woman act more like a man and hence become a better lover.

Men and women who grow in sexual sophistication along with the years find vast new vistas of sexual satisfaction in midlife. They continue to enjoy the physical pleasures of sex but do not stop there. The ability to see the person within the body, to go beyond the genitals, makes it possible for them to make more out of seemingly less.

MIND
AND
PERSONALITY

Let me caution you at the outset that we are about to tromp through a muddy field. Unlike changes in bodily functions, alterations in mental and personality attributes cannot be readily measured and studied. Entities like cardiac output and nerve conduction velocity are clearly understood, while the nature of intelligence and memory is still subject to much uncertainty and disagreement.

No one relishes the prospect of physical decline, but what truly strikes terror into the middle-aged heart is the prospect of mental deterioration, with its attendant disintegration of personality. Most of us have nothing to fear. On the contrary, in the course of the maturational process distinct benefits accrue by midlife in the realm of mind and personality.

The executive powers of the individual which reside in the mind and the personality are sustained by the brain. Yet our concepts of mind and personality cannot be fully explained by the functions of this intricate and awesome conglomerate of nerve cells. These entities are at present more readily accessible to psychological and sociological, rather than biological, methods of study.

The brain of the male, like the rest of the body, is somewhat larger than that of the female. In both sexes there is about a 10 percent reduction in brain weight between the ages of twenty and eighty. Brain weight, however, is not a reliable measure of mental competence. Other changes in the brain accompany aging, but their functional significance is also unclear. Brain cells die over time and are not replaced, but this loss does not result in any significant mental deficit during the fifties.

DEFICIT OR DIFFERENCE?

Distinct normative changes in mental functions and personality structure are in progress during the middle years. These processes in and of themselves cause no problems, although they may entail certain reductions in the efficiency of mental functions. The net effect on our daily lives depends less on the actual changes and more on how we interpret and react to them.

Deficits should not be confused with *differences* in the nature of a given function. This distinction is especially critical with respect to mental changes. There are actually fewer changes in mental functioning than in other physiological processes during the fifties. And the changes that do appear are far more difficult to document and interpret. Mental changes do not start in the fifties but are very gradual and continuous throughout adult life. Furthermore, mental changes that create a deficit often do not become apparent until the late sixties and early seventies.

Testing Mental Functions: Tests of mental functions have created much confusion about changes in cognition during the older decades. Much of the research in this area has often involved comparisons between young adults in college and the elderly in institutions because researchers have easier access to these populations. Comparing extremes makes it easier to establish differences, but the institutionalized elderly are not necessarily characteristic of their generation.

Confounding factors are another source of difficulty. The slowing down of reaction time that results from changes in nerve conduction velocity, for example, should have no bearing on functions like memory or intelligence. Yet the slower reaction time in older people conveys the impression that such mental functions decline with age, because laboratory experiments to test these functions are often time-dependent. Furthermore, these experimental situations are often quite contrived and far removed from the daily tasks confronting the elderly, so that when a deficit is demonstrated its functional or practical significance is by no means clear. In other words, the fact that an older person takes longer to put the pieces of a puzzle together may be unrelated to that person's intellectual competence on the job.

More important, there has been a shift in our conception of aging as applied to mental function. Traditional wisdom has long contended that the mind, like the body, declines with age. ("When the age is in, the wit is out" says Shakespeare in *Much Ado About Nothing*.) Early investigators of aging, who tended to follow this reasoning, ascribed the parallel decline of body and mind to the same underlying biological processes. As late as the 1950s, the prevailing view of mental development was that the first two decades were a period of positive growth and the years of later maturity a time of progressive reduction in mental efficiency. By the 1970s it was widely recognized that the mental decline of age starts later, is of lesser magnitude, and affects fewer functions than previously thought.

CHANGES IN MEMORY

Is forgetfulness the mental counterpart of gray hair? Because this is the centuries-old image of the elderly, any sign of failing memory in midlife may be ascribed to aging, even though a good deal of forgetting goes on in the younger years as well.

Faltering of the memory takes many forms: failure to recall—a name, a date, or an event; forgetting to do something—to transmit a message, pay a bill, take a pill, show up for an appointment. We may become distracted and lose our train of thought in the midst of a conversation ("What was I saying?"). These are common experiences and quite different from the pathological disturbances of memory (amnesia) that occur in conditions like Alzheimer's disease, turning the people near and dear to those afflicted into strangers. Although very few people need to be concerned about developing this disease at age fifty, many more are likely to face its devastating consequences in their parents.

Early theories conceived of memory as a way of impressing on the brain various stimuli that were then stored as bits of information in an intricate filing system available to retrieval or recall. With the development of computers and information theory, more sophisticated attempts at explaining memory that emphasize the processing of information as well as its storage have evolved.

Types of Memory: A distinction is commonly made between short-term memory and long-term memory. We think of short-term memory as referring to recent events, such as what we had for breakfast, and long-term memory as referring to what happened years ago. Yet the definitions of these terms in the research literature are quite different. In a more technical sense, short-term, or primary memory, refers to the immediate recall of events or stimuli. As soon as information leaves this ephemeral, limited-capacity storage, it enters the secondary, or long-term, memory, described as a vastly larger and more permanent storehouse of newly acquired information.

Primary memory changes very little, if at all, with aging. Slight deficits may develop by age sixty but usually not before. Problems with secondary memory, however, begin long before the middle years and are neither inevitable nor the same for all individuals. Furthermore, the decline is more marked in complex tasks such as memorizing entire paragraphs than in remembering simple sets like telephone numbers. Recall (where no cues are given) is harder than recognition (where cues are provided) and is more likely to suffer a decrease. You may have difficulty in recalling the names of your high school classmates, for example, but will have no problem matching their names to their pictures.

The common belief that the elderly have difficulty remembering recent events but are able to call to mind more distant ones led to the assumption that information is lost in reverse order of that in which it is acquired. Yet research has failed to confirm that idea. Although remote memory remains fairly intact in the older person, it is not better than the recall of more recent events; what aids the recollection of the distant past is the repetitiveness with which the elderly dwell on certain events.

With age there is a significant decline in the acquisition and recall of new information, but this decline has little practical significance for the middle-aged individual. Even in those instances when its effects become compelling in later life, their magnitude can be reduced through practicing better techniques of organization and self-regulation of the pace and methods of learning.[1]

Why should there be any loss of memory with aging? One explanation ascribes the decay of stored information to lack of use. Other hypotheses claim that memories are lost through interference—new memories crowd out the old ones, and the older you get, the greater the crowding. It is still not entirely clear whether the problem is in the acquisition of new information or in its retrieval. Studies that see the problem as one of free recall, rather than recognition, suggest that the information is still "in there" but for some reason the older person has more trouble retrieving it.

INTELLIGENCE

Intelligence is one of those concepts whose meaning is assumed intuitively, although no one can define it in a generally acceptable manner. Especially problematic is the measurement of intelligence, popularly equated with ascertaining a person's I.Q. (intelligence quotient). Consequently, when intelligence tests are used to measure age, sex, or ethnic differences, there is no end to the controversy they generate. The proponents of these tests see them as reasonably objective measures of a set of basic cognitive abilities; their opponents see them as instruments tainted by cultural bias.

Early studies suggested that people attain their maximum intelligence level in youth and that the intellect declines as they get older.

Neither of these assumptions is any longer tenable. The answer to the question, "Does intelligence decline with age?" depends on what aspect of intelligence is being measured, through what tests, and in what type of study sample.

Intelligence tests purport to measure certain fundamental cognitive processes that, once they mature, are expected to persist throughout adult life. In other words, intelligence is thought to be more or less fixed, like height; once attained it stays with you. When the Stanford-Binet intelligence test was established in 1917, a person's top I.Q. was thought to be attained by age twelve. Over the next forty years the age limit went up to twenty-one. More recently, it has been shown that peak levels are sometimes reached as late as age fifty. This shift has occurred not because adults have become smarter over successive decades, but because the ways of assessing intelligence have changed.

In earlier uses of I.Q. tests, researchers consistently found that when the intelligence scores of subjects of various ages were compared, the average I.Q. decreased with age, particularly following midlife. Such cross-sectional studies, which compare people of different generations at a given time, continue to show a significant drop in intelligence test scores around age thirty-five. Yet in longitudinal studies, which follow the progress of the same group of individuals as they grow older, test scores show a continuous climb all the way into midlife.[2]

These contradictory findings are in part due to the influence of education in each generation. During the years that these studies have been in progress, the educational level of successive generations has been rising. There is a higher proportion of college graduates among thirty-year-olds than among sixty-year-olds. Intelligence tests are heavily influenced by the level of education, as many of the test items (such as vocabulary) depend on knowledge likely to be acquired in school. Hence, older persons do worse as a group not because their brains have been turning into mush, but because they have had fewer years of schooling than the younger generations (see Figure 4-1).

Longitudinal studies avoid this pitfall. However, because the more intelligent subjects are less likely to drop out of the study, the sample becomes disproportionally weighted in favor of higher scores. Thus, while cross-sectional studies tend to underestimate the level of intelligence in older people, longitudinal studies overestimate it.

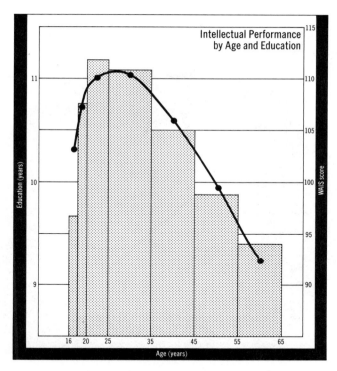

FIGURE 4-1. Vertical bar represents years of education for each age group; "points" on curve represent average Wechsler Adult Intelligence Scale (WAIS) total scale score for that group.

Intelligence used to be seen as a single, global mental entity. It is now viewed as a collection of somewhat independent factors, or a cluster of cognitive abilities such as the capacity to learn, to remember, to reason, to solve problems, and to generate new ideas. While maintaining this "omnibus" view of intelligence, investigators have attempted to differentiate between "fluid intelligence" and "crystallized intelligence." Fluid intelligence subsumes those cognitive abilities involved in the active processing of information that takes place in learning, problem solving, and the like. Crystallized intelligence is distilled out of life experiences and can be characterized as knowledge; unlike fluid intelligence, it is imbedded in a cultural context. Fluid intelligence steadily goes down throughout adult life while crystallized intelligence goes up. Omnibus intelligence, as the composite of the two, remains essentially steady over time, at least until the sixties (see Figure 4-2).

A closer look at intelligence test performance reveals further fluctuations. Intelligence tests usually have both verbal and performance

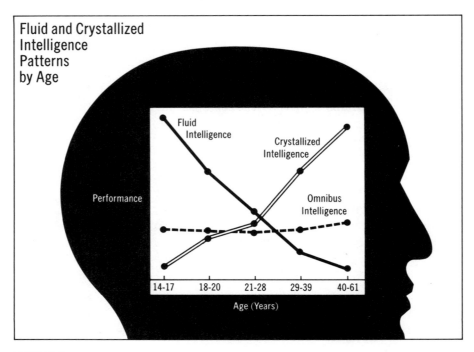

FIGURE 4-2.

components. Tests of verbal ability include the definition of words and the identification of common characteristics of objects. Verbal scores do not significantly decline with age; for persons with superior intelligence, they may actually rise. Performance scores entail the use of psychomotor skills: Instead of answering a question, the subject performs a task, such as putting a puzzle together. Unlike tests of verbal ability, performance scores are time-dependent; the faster you solve the puzzle, the higher you score. The decline of I.Q. scores among older individuals, when present, is mainly due to their poorer showing on the performance items. Given the slowing of response patterns that accompany aging, the time factor may be a critical handicap.

In practical terms, intellectual accomplishment is more significant than specific or global measures of intelligence. Intelligence is at best a potential that bears fruit under the proper environmental conditions. *Creativity* is utilized not only in the purer sense of artistic, scholarly, and scientific *productivity,* but in the more ordinary sense of what you do with what you have in everyday life. The middle years are a golden time to reap the benefits of whatever you have sown earlier in your career and daily work, as we shall see in Chapter 6.

Maintaining a Keen Edge: The capacity and the will to learn are highly important if we are to avoid obsolescence. Learning is a complex process that depends not only on memory and other cognitive factors, but also on variables such as motivation. The failure to keep on learning in midlife is more often due to the loss of motivation than to changes in mental function. If it takes an older individual somewhat longer to master difficult material, the disadvantage is more than compensated for by greater experience and a more seasoned approach to how and what to learn. For all practical purposes there is no significant diminution in learning capacity during midlife. The changes that seem to occur are more often in our subjective rather than objective perceptions of our mental abilities. Many of the differences we see when we compare ourselves to younger people can be traced to the fact that the generations following us grew up in a different educational context. It is the times rather than we that have been changing.

On the other hand, the avalanche of new information has become so overwhelming that the sense of falling farther behind as one runs faster and faster is as discouraging as the apathy that results from losing touch with the world. Therefore, the care of the mind in midlife requires not only activity but also selectivity. If older persons are at a disadvantage with respect to the former, they have a tremendous advantage over the young with respect to the latter. Having learned how to think critically, you can better sort sense from nonsense, while the young must test and try until they know their own minds.

CHANGES IN PERSONALITY

How our bodies look and our minds function has a profound impact on how others see us, but ordinarily our core identity, the basic sense of self, remains more or less intact through thick and thin.

An individual's character appears as a conglomerate of personality traits, with the more dominant traits defining the person. Yet the human personality is not only much too complex to be captured by a catalogue of adjectives, it is also far more dynamic than any static image would allow.

Whatever the psychological underpinnings of personality structure, they provide each of us with a certain constancy of character. Some of us are more sharply defined than others, but beyond a certain point we have little tolerance for individuals who are lacking in personality consistency (we label such persons as emotionally unstable or mentally ill).

Constancy of personality is important to our sense of self, as well as to our interactions with others, because it provides a measure of predictability. This consistency allows us to count on ourselves and on others to behave in expected ways in a given situation. We may or may not like these habitual behavioral patterns, but if we can predict them, we can better cope with them. Without such predictability the world of human interactions would be even more chaotic than it is. This is why we tend to deny or disregard variations from the expected pattern. When circumstances make it impossible to maintain this view, we say that a person is acting "out of character," thus permitting ourselves to maintain the conviction that the person is nonetheless who we expect him or her to be.

Aging imposes certain modifications both on one's personality and on the roles that one is expected to play. Some of these changes are adaptations to changed social circumstances, while others appear to be more independent. Whether such changes can be characterized as part of a developmental process is open to question.

Those who view personality changes as parallel to the gradual decline of biological functions are not likely to view them as part of a lifelong process of development. But life-span psychologists are more willing to press for a model of ongoing personality development involving orderly changes that are adaptive. Although there is no generally accepted theory of adult development, behavioral scientists have made a number of interesting observations on basic personality changes that men and women appear to undergo in their middle years.

ERIKSON'S SCHEME OF ADULT PERSONALITY DEVELOPMENT

The best known theory of life-span development is that of Erik Erikson.[3] In Erikson's scheme, the life cycle—the entire life span from birth to death—is characterized by eight phases of psychosocial development. Each phase is defined by the primary accomplishment of a phase-specific task, even though the resolutions are generally prepared in preceding phases and worked out further in subsequent ones.

Each phase is defined as a crisis (in the sense of a time for decision, rather than a threat of catastrophe) and labeled according to the extremes of successful and unsuccessful solutions. The actual outcome for any given individual phase, however, is generally a balance between such extremes. Theoretically there are as many gradations between the extremes as there are people.

Erikson assumes an innate ability in each individual to adapt to an "average expectable environment." Given a reasonable chance, the organism as a whole will thrive in all its specific functions. But the organism must have reasonable environmental support in order to fulfill its biological potential. This attempt at integration of biological (genetic) and environmental (societal) factors is an important aspect of Erikson's contribution to developmental theory.

Erikson views development as proceeding according to the *epigenetic principle*, whereby anything that grows has a ground plan from which its parts arise, each part having its time of special ascendancy, until all parts have arisen to form a functioning whole. This view is a reformulation of the fundamental principle that embryological development progresses from the simpler to the more complex.

Finally, there is a meshing or "cogwheeling" of the life cycles of successive generations, a crucial coordination between the needs of the nurturing representatives of society and those of the developing individual. As the infant proceeds through various phases and specific tasks, the parents, in caring for the child, master the tasks of their own phases. This mutual dependency of generations provides the necessary cohesion and impetus for the socialization of successive generations.

Even though Erikson is not locked as rigidly as Freud into the primacy of childhood, his emphasis is still on the early years. Five of his eight stages cover only the first quarter of the life span, while the long remaining period is encompassed by only three stages.

Erikson does not use the term "middle age"; what he refers to as "adulthood" seems to correspond most closely to it, as he separates young adulthood from old age. The phase-specific task for adulthood is the resolution of the psychosocial crisis of *generativity vs. stagnation.* And the human strength or ego quality that emerges from the successful negotiation of this stage is the "virtue" of *care.* Erikson defines generativity as follows:

Generativity, then, is primarily the concern in establishing and guiding the next generation, although there are individuals who, through misfortune or because of special and genuine gifts in other directions, do not apply this drive to their own offspring. And indeed, the concept of generativity is meant to include such more popular synonyms as *productivity* and *creativity*, which, however, cannot replace it.[4]

When this stage of growth fails, generativity regresses into a state of stagnation, self-absorption, and personal impoverishment. Such individuals tend to indulge themselves as if they were their own "one and only child."

Erikson's developmental stages presuppose a continuous process. In other words, the issue of generativity does not start and stop with adulthood. The successful resolution of the issue of generativity is dependent upon the work of previous stages, in particular the preceding stage of young adulthood in which the phase-specific task is intimacy vs. isolation. In this setting, generativity is usually expressed through having and rearing children, although, as Erikson makes clear, there are alternative ways of accomplishing the task of generativity, which in adulthood takes the form of *caretaking*. Erikson invokes the Hindu terms whereby adults fulfill their tasks through practicing Restraint, Charity, and Compassion, which he renders into English as "care-full," "to take care of," and "to care for."

THE SUBJECTIVE EXPERIENCE OF MIDDLE AGE

An alternative approach to studying personality change in midlife focuses on the subjective experiences of the individual. In what ways do middle-aged adults see themselves as different from the self-images they have of earlier times and their projections into later times?

This was a key question addressed by Bernice Neugarten and her associates in one of the most extensive studies of adult development, based on a sample of 700 men and women aged forty to seventy living in Kansas during the early 1960s.[5]

Neugarten does not ascribe particular changes to specific ages. Rather, she describes fundamental shifts that occur roughly between the ages of forty and sixty. Typically, age brings no sharp discontinuity in adaptational style or in personality organization. Individuals continue to cope with their internal needs and the demands of the environment through well-established habits. Nonetheless, a number of distinct shifts are apparent.

One of these shifts involves a change in time perception. During the first half of life, we tend to look back on the years we have lived. At midlife the focus shifts to time left to live. Awareness that time is limited is heightened as the prospect of death becomes more personalized.

People in midlife do not gauge their life entirely by the calendar, but look for the milestones that delineate the phase of life they are in. Someone who has reached the peak of his or her career but still has dependent children, for example, perceives the professional and the personal dimensions of life on separate scales of maturation. People in midlife see themselves as quite distinct from both younger and older generations. They constitute a bridge between the two, both within the family and in the wider contexts of work and community.[6]

The middle years bring about an increase in inner orientation or *interiority*—greater preoccupation with the inner life. Investment of the self in persons and objects in the outer world seems to decrease. People are less inclined to seek answers in the external world.

In the older years, this shift from outer-world to inner-world orientation takes the form of progressive *disengagement,* a withdrawal involving the self and society. As society delegates fewer responsibilities to aging men and women, they in turn invest less of themselves in their work and social involvements.

Disengagement is typically not a salient feature of midlife. Those who are entering their fifties usually are not yet concerned about the actual consequences of retirement or disengagement from other social roles. But psychological disengagement appears to precede by about ten years its more evident forms. Even while people continue to work, they generally experience a lessening interest and a gradual decline in drive and ambition for further accomplishment. Like many other midlife changes, inner psychological shifts help people to prepare for the more drastic shifts of the older years.

A parallel shift occurs in the style of mastery of the environment, which changes from an *active* to a *passive* mode. Forty-year-olds still believe the environment will reward initiative, risk-taking, and boldness; hence they actively seek to master it. Sixty-year-olds typically perceive the environment as complex, dangerous, and unyielding to one's wishes; hence, the self becomes more yielding and more accommodating to its demands.

These processes are accompanied by a gradual lessening of the ability to deal with complicated and challenging situations. The personality of the older self becomes less complex. There is a retreat to a set of core values and a tendency to adhere to established patterns of activity. As individuals age, they become more dogmatic in their opinions, more idiosyncratic in their reasoning, and less sensitive to the reactions of others. Their behaviors hence become more rigid and more predictable.[7]

A number of interesting differences in the personality shifts experienced by men and women become discernible at this time. Neugarten summarizes these as follows:

> Older men seem to be more receptive than younger men of their affiliative, nurturant, and sensual promptings; older women, more receptive than younger women of their aggressive and egocentric impulses. Men appear to cope with the environment in increasingly abstract and cognitive terms; women, in increasingly affective and expressive terms. In both sexes, however, older people seem to move toward more eccentric, self-preoccupied positions and to attend increasingly to the control and the satisfaction of personal needs.[8]

Like changes in mental function, changes in personality are in progress at age fifty but typically do not become quite set and salient until the decade of the sixties. Fifty-year-olds vary, of course, in the extent to which they already manifest these shifts. But even those who do not as yet exhibit these changes may become aware of them and prepare to deal with them in due time.

THE PRIME OF LIFE

Despite the heightened realization of the finitude of time and incipient shifts in personality, middle adulthood is a period when a highly differentiated self is at its peak capacity in handling a complex environment. There is a comforting feeling of knowing one's own mind and of being able to sort sense from nonsense, particularly within one's self. "Perhaps middle-age is, or should be, a period of shedding shells," writes

Anne Morrow Lindbergh, "the shell of ambition, the shell of material accumulations and possessions, and the shell of the ego."[9] Marie Dressler voices a similar view: "By the time we hit fifty, we have learned our hardest lessons. We have found out that only a few things are really important. We have learned to take life seriously, but never ourselves."[10]

This sense of proportion and perspective also comes across in the musings of Germaine Greer on midlife:

> You care about yourself less and less. Your vanity and pride stop getting in your way. You begin to develop a sense of proportion . . . you stop squandering emotion on foolish things . . . or waste time on fatuities. You can escape from the dominion of your own passions and enter into a calm wherein you can fix your eye upon a worthy objective and pursue it wholeheartedly.[11]

Fifty is the time for hearing the voice of *wisdom*, notwithstanding H.L. Mencken ("The older I grow the more I distrust the familiar doctrine that age brings wisdom.") In our modern world, the word *wisdom* has a quaint ring to it, but what it stands for remains as vital today as it has been throughout history. Through wisdom, as distinguished from knowledge, we are able to be discerning in judgment and to seek answers not only to "why?" and "how?" but also "what for?"

Many fifty-year-olds have good reason to think of themselves in highly favorable terms. They may well miss some aspects of being younger, but very few express the wish to be young again; although they do not fear getting old, they are glad not to be old yet. The self is now a well-tuned instrument that does one's bidding, adding to one's sense of competence and autonomy. In summarizing their findings with respect to the subjective experience of middle age, Neugarten and Datan write:

> In pondering the data on these men and women, we have been impressed with the central importance of what might be called the excecutive processes of personality in middle age: self-awareness, selectivity, manipulation and control of the environment, mastery, competence, the wide array of cognitive strategies. We are impressed, too, with reflection as a striking characteristic of the mental life of middle-aged

persons: the stocktaking, the heightened introspection, and above all, the structuring and restructuring of experience—that is, the conscious processing of new information in the light of what one has already learned and the turning of one's proficiency to the achievement of desired ends. These people feel that they effectively manipulate their social environments on the basis of prestige and expertise; and that they create many of their own rules and norms. There is a sense of increased control over impulse life. The middle-aged person often describes himself as no longer "driven," but as the "driver"—in short, "in command."[12]

STRESS AND STABILITY

The psychological state of the midlife individual is characterized by two seemingly contradictory images. One image is that of a psychologically mature person who projects a picture of health and calm self-assurance, content with and in control of one's self. The other image is that of the fretful and depressed menopausal woman or the anxious and conflicted man going through the midlife crisis. There is an element of reality in both alternatives, depending on the personality of the individual and the particular circumstances of midlife that he or she is experiencing.

The Midlife Transition: The midlife transition, or the *midlife crisis*, is generally thought to take place sometime in the forties. As currently described, it is experienced mainly by men. In some ways it constitutes the psychosocial counterpart of the female climacteric; some in fact equate it with a "male menopause," and ascribe to it a wide variety of symptoms ranging from nervousness, depression, and indecisiveness to loss of sexual interest, lack of self-confidence, and a variety of other symptoms.[13]

There is as yet, however, no evidence of a fundamental biological reason for the midlife crisis. Rather, it is the career-based pattern of male lives that seems to be primarily responsible for its manifestations. As more women follow traditionally male career paths, it will be interesting to see if they too become vulnerable to the same conflicts.

The causes of the midlife crisis are multiple and varied, but usually it is their cumulative effect that precipitates the crisis. The challenges that lead up to a crisis may be stretched out over a decade or more. As Orville Brim sums it up,

> A "male mid-life crisis" will occur for some men if there are multiple simultaneous demands for personality change; if, for instance, during the same month or year the man throws off his last illusions about great success; accepts his children for what they are; buries his father and his mother and yields to the truth of his mortality; recognizes that his sexual vigor and, indeed, interest, are declining, and even finds relief in the fact.
>   . . . . These challenges may be stretched out over ten or twenty years. Some men are obsessed about their achievements, but not yet confronting the fact of death; other men are sharply disappointed in their children's personalities but not yet concerned about sexual potency. The events come early for some men, much later for others. There is no evidence that they are related to chronological age in any but the most general sense, e.g., "sometime during the forties."[14]

Daniel Levinson reckons that the majority (about 80 percent) of midlife men go through a time of moderate or severe crisis between the ages of forty and forty-five.[15] The rest go through midlife without experiencing any significant distress. Some of them are able to evade the issues at hand by bypassing reassessment of the meaning, value, and direction of their lives. They presumably go through the midlife transition at a later date or settle for a stunted development.

The midlife transition seen in this perspective is not only a normal experience but a necessary step in moving through middle age. It is fundamentally a process of stocktaking followed by adjustments in a number of key areas. Why is it, then, so turbulent? Why shouldn't stocktaking be a time of rejoicing? If they are happily married, their children successively launched—or happily single, enjoying the peak of their careers—why should people in their forties be wringing their hands?

The answer is that stocktaking implies the possibility of change; change disturbs the equilibrium of our lives and hence is stressful. The emotional economy of life sustains the routines of our existence even if they are less than satisfactory. Having made it to midlife, most of us are by now either happy with or resigned to who we are, what we do, and those with whom we are intimately associated. Rocking the boat provokes anxiety. This tendency to maintain the status quo is further reinforced by our close associates. Unless you are so obnoxious that any change would be for the better, the people that you live with and work with have a vested interest in keeping you as you are, considering the time and energy they have spent learning to deal with you.

Why then do we insistently go through this midlife auditing? One reason is that we have established stability at a substantial cost in freedom and fulfillment. Even if we have done well, we still ask ourselves, "Is this as well as I could have done?" and also, "Is this really what I wanted to do?"

The specifics of each person's concerns reflect the realities of that person's life. But there are also a number of general issues that inevitably confront us during the midlife transition. Levinson defines these in terms of a set of polarities that must be renegotiated as part of the process of midlife *individuation*. These polarities involve the following dimensions: young and old, masculine and feminine, destructiveness and creativeness, attachment and separateness.

The Residues of Midlife Transition: By age fifty, most of us have presumably gone through the midlife transition. With respect to the young-old polarity, there is a redefinition of where we fall in the spectrum not only in chronological terms but also in psychological and social terms. Some fifty-year-olds act much younger or much older than others.

The gender reorientation is closely related to the tendency for men and women to become more alike in midlife. Traditionally, men were supposed to be more authoritarian, self-assertive, competitive, and independent, while women were expected to be submissive, dependent, and nurturant. Such images have always been true only in a very general sense; one could always find some individuals who did not conform to these stereotypes. Furthermore, such expectations are culturally defined and subject to change. Nonetheless, within these limitations, the shift with age is toward a more common gender pattern. Some ascribe this shift to the surfacing of personality traits that have been suppressed earlier: Age allows the feminine side of men and the masculine side of women greater freedom of expression and visibility.

The issues of destructiveness and creativeness are particularly salient at this time. By the time we have reached middle age, many of us wield considerable influence on our families and our co-workers. The way we use that power may be creative or destructive. Our basic stance must now be redefined. The same kind of choice applies to attachment and separateness in our friendships, the extent to which we live for others or for ourselves, and—perhaps most important—in redefining our relationships with our children, spouses, and parents.

ADAPTATION
TO LIFE

There are many ways of defining mental health, but a key ingredient in any definition is the capacity to adapt to and cope with the vicissitudes of life. No matter how privileged the individual and fortunate the circumstances of his or her life, everyone must contend with inevitable losses, stresses, and conflicts.

Every phase of life has its particular challenges, sorrows, and joys. Though we think of some periods of life—adolescence, for example— as being more difficult than others, such judgments are relative and highly variable from one person to another. Nor is aging as such a reason for inevitable distress. As Plato stated long ago, "He who is of a calm and happy nature will hardly feel the pressure of age, but to him who is of an opposite disposition youth and age are equally a burden." The maturational process nonetheless entails certain shifts in the use of the ego's *defense mechanisms* through which the person reconciles the requirements of the inner self with the demands of the outer world.

Defense mechanisms vary in their adaptive usefulness and hence may lead to either mature or neurotic behaviors. The more mature and healthy ego defenses include the mechanisms of *anticipation* (thinking ahead to cope with the consequences of stressful events), *sublimation* (expressing socially problematic urges in acceptable yet still pleasurable forms), *suppression* (conscious renunciation or postponement of problematic desires), and *altruism* (performing gratifying service to others).

By contrast, neurotic mechanisms lead to solutions that are less adaptive. Repression, for example, allows a person to remain unaware that he or she harbors certain unacceptable thoughts and feelings that influence behavior. Or, through the use of *dissociation*, one may "split off" an unacceptable part of the self and behave in an inconsistent or unpredictable manner. *Intellectualization* detaches thoughts from their appropriate feelings, while *reaction formation* twists behaviors into their opposites. Yet other mechanisms distort reality in more serious ways. *Projection*, for instance, ascribes one's own unacceptable feelings to others and can lead to the formation of delusions of persecution.

Between the ages of thirty-five and fifty, mature defenses come to be used more frequently. Among subjects studied, men in middle life were four times as likely to use mature as immature defenses.[16] With maturity there is a decline in the use of fantasy and acting out in impulsive and self-indulgent ways. All of the more mature defenses, especially suppression, are more heavily relied on, at the expense of some of the neurotic and immature defenses. Central to all these shifts is the capacity to integrate, to make sense of experience, and to become whole.

So this is the time to come to terms with yourself: To identify the truly unacceptable in you, isolate it, and keep it in check—in your heart as well as in your behavior. You will thereby unlock the prisoners of conscience that you have unfairly incarcerated and allow yourself to live more fully than you have ever done before.

The willingness to grow throughout life is the antidote to the stagnation of age. But so is the ability to stay put and to say, "This is who I am, and this is who I will remain." Some people are constantly trying to improve their game. But there is a time, and age fifty is as good a time as any, to stop practicing and start playing, to stop rehearsing and start performing, to stop planning and start living.

5

KITH
AND
KIN

Our lives are shaped by our families. Not only does virtually everyone grow up in a family, but the great majority of people establish families of their own. Close to 95 percent of the American population has been married at least once before age fifty. The fact that we have living parents, siblings, or adult children does not always mean that we have significant ties with them, but for most of us, the most important relationships throughout our lives continue to be with the members of our families.

DEMOGRAPHIC REALITIES

Among Americans in the forty-five to fifty-four age group, 81 percent of the men and 74 percent of the women are married and living with their spouses. An additional 3 percent of men and 4 percent of women are married but living apart from their spouses. Most often these couples are estranged; less often the spouse is absent for career or other reasons.

The unmarried minority of this age group consists of the divorced (11 percent of the women, 9 percent of the men); the widowed (6 percent of the women, 1 percent of the men); and the single or never married (6 percent of the men, 5 percent of the women).[1]

An American woman born in 1900 could expect to live only until age sixty-four. She would typically have married at about age twenty-two a man of twenty-six, been widowed by age sixty, and died before her last child left home. Today, a fifty-year-old woman has three more decades of life ahead of her.

Ages at first marriage declined steadily from the turn of the century until 1960, when the median age for men had dropped to twenty-three and for women to twenty. During the last two decades, the trend has reversed itself, and couples have been getting married progressively later, so that in the mid-1980s, ages at first marriage for both sexes approximate the figures in 1890. Among men, the highest rate of marriage is in the twenty-five to twenty-nine age group (140 marriages per 1000 unmarried population in 1980). The rate for those forty-five to fifty-four is about half that of those twenty-five to twenty-nine. Among women, the highest rate is in the twenty to twenty-four bracket, 139 per 1000 unmarried population in 1980 (see Figure 5-1).

Women now tend to stop having children much earlier than their grandmothers did, and a mother's last child leaves home at eighteen. A fifty-year-old woman now faces a stretch of approximately thirty

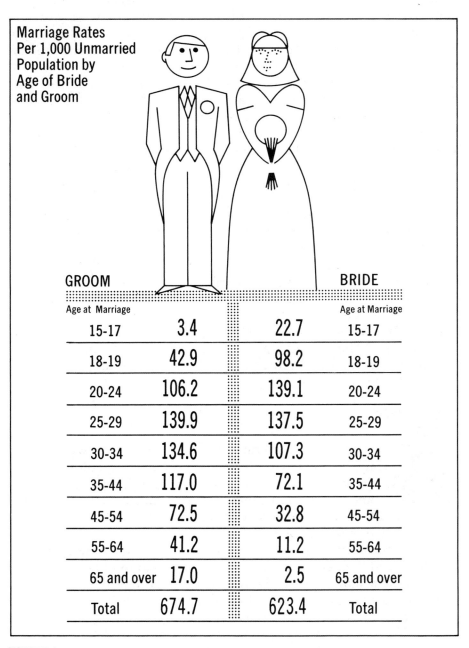

Marriage Rates
Per 1,000 Unmarried
Population by
Age of Bride
and Groom

GROOM Age at Marriage			BRIDE Age at Marriage
15-17	3.4	22.7	15-17
18-19	42.9	98.2	18-19
20-24	106.2	139.1	20-24
25-29	139.9	137.5	25-29
30-34	134.6	107.3	30-34
35-44	117.0	72.1	35-44
45-54	72.5	32.8	45-54
55-64	41.2	11.2	55-64
65 and over	17.0	2.5	65 and over
Total	674.7	623.4	Total

FIGURE 5-1.

years of postparental life. In all probability her husband will survive until she is sixty-nine, which will leave her with sixteen years of widowhood. But there is a 50 percent chance that her first marriage will have ended in divorce long before her husband dies. In many instances, therefore, a married woman will become a widow or a divorcee by the time she is forty-four years old and, unless she remarries, she will retain that status for thirty-six years. If she does remarry, let us say at age forty-five, she will spend part of the next thirty-five years with her second husband. Since he is likely to be older than she by a wider margin than was her first husband, she now has an even chance of losing him through death or divorce within eleven years, when she still has twenty-six years of life remaining.[2]

Very few people marry for the first time in their fifties. Many more remarry in midlife. The marriage rate for women aged forty-five to fifty-four years is, however, only one-fourth that of the peak years, and less than half that of men forty-five to fifty-four. Clearly, men in this age group are more likely to marry than women, and this pattern becomes even more exaggerated in later years: In the fifty-five to sixty-four age group, the marriage rate is almost four times higher for men than for women; among those sixty-five and older, it is seven times higher.[3] These demographic realities are at the root of some of the most important differences in the lives and marital prospects of men and women at midlife.

THE MARRIED
AT FIFTY

Being married, preferably to the same person with whom you began married life, remains an abiding cultural ideal, even though an increasingly larger proportion of men and women have found that ideal difficult to sustain. For the three out of four individuals who remain married at fifty, how does the institution of marriage work?

In an ideal scenario, a highly compatible man and woman start life together, and their subsequent development as individuals, as a couple, and as a family proceeds in synchrony so that over time their bonds grow stronger and their lives become increasingly more complementary. For couples in a reasonably happy marriage the decade of the fifties is a wonderful time. In a traditional relationship, the husband is well established in his work and has a realistic appraisal of the remaining course of his career. Secure and competent in his job, he can now turn more of his attention to his family; with the children gone, that means mainly his wife. She has, in turn, successfully discharged her childrearing responsibilities and now has ample time to pursue her own interests and spend more time with her husband. After many years, they are once again a couple on their own. They may settle down to a quiet and comfortable life, or choose a life-style of adventure and travel. Now is the time to do all of those things they have been hoping to do "someday."

The current pattern is somewhat different. Half of all married women now work outside the home, either to increase the family income or for the satisfaction of facing new challenges and exploring new opportunities. Women who have been working all along, juggling job and family, can now either turn their full attention to their careers or gain a greater measure of leisure and freedom to pursue other interests.

Husband and wife in these relationships can develop a greater sense of partnership and parity in midlife. Typically they have more time, more money, and more freedom than ever before. And there are several decades of life ahead to enjoy and to prepare for the requirements of old age.

Interactions with parents and children provide additional sources of fulfillment. With their children successfully launched, parents have the pleasure of watching them become established in their careers and form their own families. Midlife parents have the satisfaction of seeing their own parents enjoy the fruits of their labors in happy retirement. Friendship now complements filial and parental bonds.

These rather idyllic circumstances may be compromised on one or another front. The children may have problems in their work or love relationships. Elderly parents may be ill or financially unprepared for retirement. The marriage itself may break up after years of unhappiness or develop new tensions because of the changing circumstances of the couple's lives. Couples who appear mismatched at the outset sometimes make a success of their partnership while marriages seemingly made in heaven flounder. Either outcome is possible because people change over time at different rates and in different directions. The two main factors that make or break a marriage are therefore marital choice and the evolution of the marital relationship.
Marital Choice: Though choosing a mate is typically a task of younger adulthood, the choice is equally important when people remarry

during midlife. In our idealized image, a couple falls in love, gets married, and lives happily ever after. In reality, while a certain degree of affection figures in most decisions to get married, falling in love is neither a prerequisite nor necessarily the best basis for marriage. And, although middle-aged people remain perfectly capable of falling in love, they are less likely to expect a full-blown romance.

Being in love, as distinguished from *loving someone* in a more settled and enduring manner, is a transient experience with a distinct onset and a predictable course.[4] It is sustained by the processes of *idealization* (whereby the crooked nose of the beloved appears straight) and *crystallization* (which makes the crooked nose look cute). When in full force there is a constant preoccupation with the love object and an acute longing for the reciprocation of one's affection. When love is returned, the person feels exhilarated ("walking on air"). The prospect of rejection induces doubt, confusion, frustration, and "heartache." (Arabian physicians in the eighth century called love madness *ishik,* after a creeper that winds around a tree and chokes it to death; the traditional Western image for marriage is a vine clustered around an elm.) Sexual attraction is a basic ingredient of being in love, although sexual fulfillment is by no means the key concern for most people who are in love.

The process of choosing a marital partner is more prosaic, though it is not without its romantic and affectional elements. Generally, the first step is an interest in getting married, which leads one to actively seek a mate or, more passively, to make oneself available. Preliminary attraction to a potential mate is based on readily visible attributes, such as physical features, poise, gregariousness, similarities of interest, and tentative appraisals of how closely the person fits one's ideal of a spouse.

As a man and woman begin to move within their respective social circles, the reactions of others and their being identified as a couple help to formalize the relationship. As a feeling of comfort in each other's presence grows, self-disclosure leads to a greater sense of intimacy and rapport. The affectional bond gets stronger still as each person finds validation by the other of his or her deeper values and aspirations. Level of emotional maturity and commitment are now scrutinized more closely. Differences in ethnicity, religious affiliation, social class, and other variables are confronted more directly. If the net effect is the reciprocal feeling that "this is right for me" or the recognition that "this is the best I can do," then the matter is settled.[5]

This sequence makes the choice of a mate appear to be more rational or more calculated than the process we have experienced—and are willing to admit. While it may be true that some people get married at a time when marriage is the last thing on their minds, custom and convention also lead us to feign disinterest in the prospect of marriage unless it happens "naturally" and almost despite ourselves. It is more romantic to think that the right person induced us to consider marriage. Few admit to seduction and scheming to get a mate.

Similarly, although we think of ourselves as highly autonomous in choosing a spouse, the dominant pattern in marriage is one of *homogamy*, meaning that people generally choose others who are more or less similar to themselves in social, psychological, and physical assets and characteristics. Where there are marked disparities, some compensatory mechanism tends to balance things out. An attractive man, for example, may marry a less attractive woman of a higher social class, or vice versa.

We commonly ascribe marital unhappiness to couples having made poor choices. As a result, when people decide to separate, the typical reaction is that they made a mistake in getting married to each other. But it may well be that the couple constituted a good match on their wedding day but drifted apart in incompatible directions.

In other cases, the seeds of disenchantment are indeed sown when a marital partner is chosen. If one is still uncertain about his or her own identity as an individual when making the choice, there is only a slim chance of making a good match; consequently many teenage marriages do not survive. If we rush into a choice when we are temporarily unsettled, perhaps on the rebound from a divorce, the person we get may not be the one we need. Even under stable circumstances, the incentive to get the best deal rather than the best *fit* will cause problems. The potential spouse with the highest "value" by objective standards in the marriage market may not be the best choice in any given case.

Choosing a spouse is in some ways like buying clothes. When a man is trying on a new suit he tends to stand straight, but, having bought the suit, he lapses into his usual slouch and the suit no longer fits him properly. Women too put their best foot forward during courtship, conveying an equally erroneous impression, which soon enough yields to the reality of who they are.

While there is no evidence that the process of mate selection becomes fundamentally different at age fifty, one would expect some differences in the characteristics sought in a marital partner. Mature people are expected to make more level-headed judgments and to be less susceptible to momentary passions. Physical attractiveness may be less important than good health, compatability of character more important than social status.

The Course of Marriages: The Czech writer Milan Kundera likens the evolution of an intimate relationship to the composition of a symphony with its various movements. Those who stay together long enough jointly compose an entire work. Those who do not stay together leave behind partly finished works, or a series of short pieces, but either alternative may result in a happy outcome. Those with many partners leave behind discordant compositions, while those who stay in unhappy relationships can be compared to records in which the needle has gotten stuck.

How do intact marriages evolve into the middle years? Very few formal studies shed light on this process from a longitudinal perspective. Various and sundry sources provide a variety of interpretations. One can hypothesize a number of pathways whereby marriages are consolidated over time or gradually run out of steam. Yet there is no consistent pattern into which the evolution of all marriages can be fitted.

When we look at successful marital relationships, one type of happy marriage is based on companionship characterized by mutual affection and the expression of love, open communication, and respect. Other happy marriages are founded on a mutuality of emotional and material investments. These two alternatives are, of course, not mutually exclusive. Often the ties of companionship are further cemented over the years as couples accumulate children, possessions, and life experiences together.

Global judgments of marital satisfaction are particularly difficult to make, because a couple is likely to be happy in one phase of the marriage and unhappy in another. Some do fine until they have children but then cannot handle parenthood; in other marriages the birth of children cements a faltering relationship.

The passage of time generally brings about greater intimacy, but this is by no means an inevitable outcome. Following an initial period of intensive self-revelation and interaction, many spouses settle into a level of communication that is primarily geared to the requirements of everyday life. Having skimmed the surface, they have no further desire—nor do they have the ability—to explore in greater depth who the other person is. Or a process of alienation gradually turns the intimates of yesterday into the strangers of today. A partner who was an asset in youth may become a burden in midlife.

Long-term relationships are forged by *attraction* and *attachment*. While these two processes typically reinforce one another, they are not identical and do not always coexist. Early in a relationship couples are highly attracted to each other because of the novelty of the relationship and the presence of various positive factors. But there is as yet no opportunity for a deeper attachment to form. Breakups occur more easily at this stage, as attraction wanes and people shift their attention to others.

Over the course of time, the bonds of attachment are expected to become stronger through the sharing of life experiences and progressive dependence on each other. While continuing attraction facilitates this process, there may also be an inverse relationship in which attachment grows as attraction erodes. The paradox of two people continuing to live together even though there is very little attraction left, or despite a great deal of animosity, is explicable on the basis of attachment outlasting attraction.

We think of love, respect, and other positive emotions as the binding forces between husband and wife. Yet negative emotions may also exert a strong pull in keeping two individuals together despite discord and misery. Some couples are married to each other for decades even though their communications barely go beyond the requirements necessitated by living under the same roof. True, some people persist in unhappy marriages because of compelling circumstances. But others persist in their neurotic need to inflict or suffer unhappiness.

Even in the best of matrimonial pairings, there are shifts in the marital relationship over time. These shifts must be understood in terms of both what weakens the marriage and what strengthens it. It is easy enough to see that certain forms of behavior—hostility, dishonesty, failure to fulfill one's obligations—are inimical. But it is not enough to refrain from doing anything "bad"; spouses must constantly do something "good" to counteract the process of decay that can gradually degrade the quality of a marriage.

Researchers have studied some of these processes to observe the personal development undergone by husbands and wives over the years and to find out how those changes affect the marriage. When husband and wife start with a reasonably good match and do not significantly change in their personalities and life aspirations, the relationship is likely to remain satisfactory to both. The addition of children may alter and tax the relationship somewhat, but after the children have left home, these couples typically resume earlier levels of satisfaction, thus experiencing a second honeymoon.

If one partner changes, but the other remains the same, the marital relationship may deteriorate, either because the changing partner's new needs are not being satisfied or because he or she is no longer willing or able to satisfy the continuing needs of the stable partner. When husband and wife change simultaneously, the marriage itself may evolve and continue to be highly satisfying, albeit in different ways than before. On the other hand, if the spouses change in opposite directions, maximum tension and disruption result.

The impact of marriage and parenting is quite different for men and women. The traditional pattern of marital relationships continues among most modern couples. Even though more wives are working outside the home, work has by no means freed them from primary responsibility for child rearing and housekeeping. A 1976 study of female physicians conducted in Detroit showed that three-fourths of these women were doing all the cooking, shopping, child care, and money management for their families; a third of them also did all the laundry and heavy cleaning.[6] No wonder more husbands than wives find marriage satisfactory. Even men who claim to be dissatisfied with their marriages are typically reflecting unhappiness with their overall life situation, particularly with their jobs or their children, rather than with their relationships with their wives.

After all is said and done, the critical factor in marital satisfaction seems to be the determination to make the marriage work. There is a curious circularity in this observation. Those who try hardest at making their marriage work do so because they see some value in the marriage; but at the same time, because they invest so much effort, they make their marriage more valuable to themselves.

Renewing the Marriage: The greater sense of interiority at midlife should lead you to spend more meaningful time with yourself. But unless you intend to free your soul through asceticism, greater interiority does not mean shutting yourself off from other people. Midlife is a time for cultivating not only the self but also kith and kin, beginning with your spouse if you have one. The exigencies of marriage and parenthood that bond husband and wife over the years are curiously insulating. We stand so close together that we cannot see each other. When the children are more or less independent, and the maintenance of work and family has become stabilized, married couples have a particularly good opportunity to get reacquainted and to synchronize their lives for the years ahead.

If your marriage has survived for twenty or thirty years, there is much to be said for preserving it. If the relationship has been less than idyllic, familiarity and routine have taken much of the excitement out of it, and potential new mates beckon, you may be tempted to consider making a new start. But think twice before you do.

If the fabric is sound, it is generally better to fix a marriage that has been part of you for so long rather than replace it. It is easier to get reacquainted than to cultivate a brand new relationship, exciting as that prospect may appear. You will be surprised how much of you is tied up in your wife or husband of many years and how large the gap will be in your life if you wrench that part of you away.

The sun blazes as brightly in the afternoon as in the morning but it will not last as long. As a fifty-year-old, you may even consider yourself better equipped than a younger person to be a spouse. But enduring ties take time to build and you do not have as much time as a younger person.

Revitalizing a marriage requires openness, ingenuity, compassion, and realism. It is like renegotiating a contract with a clear assessment of the assets and liabilities of its continuation. But remember that *renegotiating* a contract is not the same as *negotiating* a new one. An old contract has a past; a new one does not. The life the couple has shared, their children, friends, the assets they hold in common—all of these are considerations that cannot be swept aside in the rush to make a clean start. By giving up all you may lose as much as will the spouse you are leaving.

The renewal of the marital relationship is an ongoing process and not limited to any one age or transitional period. But in addition to its daily maintenance, marriage also requires major periodic over-hauling, and the middle of midlife is a good time for it.

In trying to convert principles of renewal into practice, remember that the symbolic is no less important than the substantive if it expresses your true feelings. There are numerous ways to indicate that a change is afoot, that you sincerely wish to get close to your partner, for who she or he *is*, not for what he or she *does* for you. This process of rapprochement in midlife must be a mutual process, a two-way street. Spouses may express their affection and reward each other in different ways, but the intentions behind the deeds and the magnitude of the effort should be symmetrical.

TERMINATING THE MARRIAGE

Marriages that have survived into the middle years deserve a second chance. But a seriously ailing marriage need not be nursed indefinitely. Commitments must be honored, yet to stay married simply because one has been married for so long may not be sufficient justification for the suffering people inflict on each other in an unhappy relationship.

Marital relationships are sometimes damaged beyond repair—"the plate is broken," they say in the Middle East—or the emotional cost of maintaining the marriage mounts so high that life becomes intolerable. Therefore, if conscientious efforts to renew the marriage fail, a case can be made for divorcing in midlife. No one can tell you when the point of no return has been reached. Nor can you always be absolutely certain that you are making the right decision. The paralysis that results from not knowing what to do is as unfortunate as the rashness with which some throw their marriages away. A certain measure of uncertainty and ambivalence is unavoidable under these circumstances; you cannot always be sure of how you feel, and it is even harder to tell how you are likely to feel a year, or ten years, from now.

To make sure that your decision will be as rational and realistic as possible, ask yourself if you would rather be unmarried than stay in your present marriage. To be unmarried is an option that is available to you; a better marriage is only a hope. There is nothing wrong in hoping as long as you do not count on its fulfillment in exchange for giving up what you have.

Having reconciled yourself to the thought of possibly remaining unmarried you must next assess in as realistic terms as possible what being unmarried is going to mean to you—emotionally, sexually, socially, financially, and in other significant ways. Finally, consider how a divorce would affect your spouse and children. If the anticipated unhappiness of others would be drastically greater than the anticipated improvement in your own happiness, you may decide not to go through with it but to make the best of the situation. You must be careful, however, not to make your life a hostage to someone else's sentiments or to be manipulated by his or her needs.

Only you can assess the degrees of happiness and unhappiness anticipated or where to draw the line between decent and compassionate behavior and masochistic suffering.

THE UNMARRIED AT FIFTY

Because being married is considered by our society as the normative state, we relegate a substantial portion of the population to a negatively defined category when we refer to them as *un*married, even though many of these individuals may be single by choice rather by default. The current use of the term "single" to subsume the divorced, the separated, the widowed, and the never-married can be confusing, as it has traditionally been used to designate the last category only.

There are obvious and important differences among the component groups in this category. The never-married bachelor, the thrice-married divorced man, and the widow who has not remarried are apt to have widely differing life circumstances and marital prospects. They do, however, share an important feature—not having a spouse—which has equally important repercussions on their lives.

The Divorced in Midlife: Among those forty-five to fifty-four, approximately one out of ten women (11 percent) and a somewhat smaller proportion of men (8 percent) are divorced. The divorce rate, on the increase for the last sixty years, rose sharply following World War II, and has accelerated markedly during the last two decades. For white women, marriages ending in divorce went up from 14 percent between 1940 and 1945 to 45 percent between 1975 and 1980; for black women, the rates rose even higher, making them the most likely group in the United States to be divorced.

Among both men and women, divorce rates peak in the twenty-five to twenty-nine age group and decline markedly with the approach of middle age (see Figure 5-2). In 1980, for men of fifty to fifty-four, there were 22,517 divorces, which is only one-fifth of the annual number in the peak years. For women in the same age group, there were 15,722 divorces, which is one-eighth the annual number in the peak years.[7]

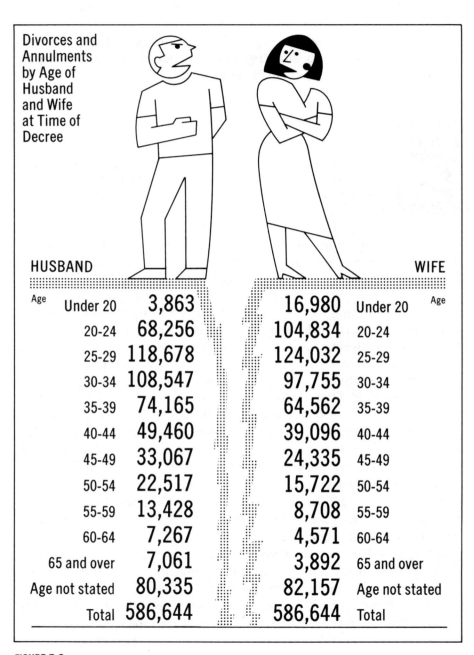

Divorces and Annulments by Age of Husband and Wife at Time of Decree

HUSBAND				WIFE
Age				Age
Under 20	3,863	16,980	Under 20	
20-24	68,256	104,834	20-24	
25-29	118,678	124,032	25-29	
30-34	108,547	97,755	30-34	
35-39	74,165	64,562	35-39	
40-44	49,460	39,096	40-44	
45-49	33,067	24,335	45-49	
50-54	22,517	15,722	50-54	
55-59	13,428	8,708	55-59	
60-64	7,267	4,571	60-64	
65 and over	7,061	3,892	65 and over	
Age not stated	80,335	82,157	Age not stated	
Total	586,644	586,644	Total	

FIGURE 5-2.

The timing of divorce has remained essentially the same over the years; it is still most common during the early years of marriage. Age at marriage is also quite significant. Men who marry before twenty-one and women who marry before twenty are most likely to divorce. Two-thirds of women whose first marriages break up are divorced by age thirty.

Couples with low incomes, couples who have children soon after marriage, and couples with divorced parents (who tend to marry others with divorced parents) are most likely to divorce. College graduates, couples with high incomes, and those born earlier in the century have the lowest divorce rates.

Why do people get divorced? The answers to that question are as obvious, and sometimes as mystifying, as the answers to the question, Why do people stay married? The answers are lodged in the choice of the mate and the evolution of the relationship. Some marriages are so seriously defective that they can't survive for long. Other marriages sooner or later yield to the wear and tear of living together.

Some couples have more to contend with than others. But more important, couples who stay together have found effective means of repairing and reviving the relationship. Much also depends on one's expectations. The more unrealistic and infantile one's needs, the less likely they are to be fulfilled, no matter who the spouse is.

For a sound marriage to go suddenly sour at midlife would be highly unusual. Most couples who get divorced in midlife admit that they have had problems for a long time but had postponed divorce until the circumstances of their lives had changed in some way— often by the departure of their children. But it would be an oversimplification to say that these marriages were held together by the children. Parents are rightly concerned about the impact of divorce on their children, but parenthood is only one of the reasons why some troubled marriages stay together.

In the most unhappy case, a mismatched couple makes the worst of a bad situation and suffers chronic turmoil, or is resigned to a life of quiet despair. Others go through a succession of bad marriages, each compounding the mistakes of the former. By the time these people reach fifty, they are usually cynical about marriage. Yet it is not always possible to understand why some unhappy marriages remain intact while seemingly less troubled marriages break up. As Tolstoy observed, "All happy families resemble one another, but each unhappy family is unhappy in its own way."

Unless she prefers a single life, a middle-aged woman should think twice before dissolving a marriage, for age is a particularly serious impediment to her remarriage. A woman divorced in her twenties has a 76 percent chance of remarriage. With each successive decade that figure decreases: to 56 percent in her thirties; 32 percent in her forties; and 12 percent in her fifties and beyond.[8]

Middle-aged men fare better in the remarriage market, especially if they are well off, well educated, and in a prestigious profession. Ninety percent of such men are married at any given time. By contrast, professional success seems to be an added impediment to the remarriage of women: Women with postgraduate degrees and personal incomes of about $20,000 in 1977 had four times the divorce rate of women with lesser achievements outside the home and a 20 percent greater likelihood of never remarrying (especially those who had a relatively late first marriage).

Being divorced no longer carries the stigma that it once did. Yet the process remains quite stressful, and the task of resocialization into the role of a single person is not always easy. Unlike marriage, which entails traditional guidelines as to how to function in the role of husband or wife, divorce is not yet similarly institutionalized. Being single after divorce is quite different from being not yet married. Among other considerations, there is the former spouse, children, mutual friends, and a shared past with which the divorced person must come to terms.

Dealing with former spouses continues to occupy much time and energy until there is a realignment of lives and an establishment of new links. While these postdivorce interactions tend to be turbulent (most often because of arguments over money), they are by no means all negative. Old affections may persist, although laced with ambivalence. (Quite a few former spouses continue to engage in sexual intercourse together during the months following divorce.) For many others, the former spouse remains a significant figure to whom they turn in times of crisis. And the common investment in the children requires ongoing collaboration.

In some ways, divorce is harder on the middle-aged, and its problems are different for men and women. In the period immediately following the divorce, men over fifty have a particularly difficult time; having depended on their wives for years, they must now learn to look after themselves. By contrast, the most distressed among women are those divorced in their twenties.

In the long run, however, it is the divorced older woman who has the hardest time. Many of her problems are financial. Homemaking is still the primary occupation of a majority of married women in their middle years. They have invested their time and energies in raising children and taking care of their families. Typically, their vocational skills are not well developed even if they have graduated from college, and, if they have ever been employed, their work experiences have probably been sporadic.

Reforms in divorce laws have sometimes helped and sometimes worked to the detriment of women. In the year following her divorce, a woman's standard of living now declines by an average 73 percent while the man's rises by 42 percent.[9] Middle-aged divorced women are not eligible for social security benefits because they are too young. They do not qualify for federal welfare programs if they are not physically disabled and if their children are over eighteen. Having worked in their homes, they cannot collect unemployment insurance. They cannot benefit from the pension and health plans of their former husbands. When they look for jobs, their age, sex, and lack of work experience are likely to be disadvantages.

Psychological and social considerations further complicate the lives of these women. Their identities, roles, status, and social networks have been determined largely by their husbands and by their identification as a couple. So for many of them, being suddenly on their own feels like having the rug pulled out from under their feet. These women are aptly called "displaced homemakers" because they are like refugees in their own country. To say that they are "under-employed, underpaid, underfinanced, underhoused, undervalued, and underloved" may be overstating the case, but their plight is real enough.[10]

We must be careful, however, not to generalize these rather grim prospects to all women who get divorced in midlife. Consider the forty-eight-year-old attractive and accomplished physician on the faculty of a major medical school. Her long-standing marriage has gradually run out of steam. Her two children are in college. The divorce is mutually agreed upon and amicable. She faces none of the burdens enumerated above. On the contrary, the prospect of being free of the constricting relationship is a source of relief, and the future is full of promise for her professionally and personally.

A middle-aged woman whose husband left her with no assets except their house became interested in the real estate business in order to sell her house more advantageously. She turned out to be so adept at it that she was soon selling real estate and prospering. In countless less dramatic examples, women who fashion new lives for themselves, despite the hurts and hardships, feel better off than when they were married.

Divorced women may also find—usually much to their surprise—that they like living alone once they've grown accustomed to it. There is a feeling of release from the tension of living with unresolved conflicts. After years of stress within the home, one's apartment or house is now a refuge, a place for peaceful rest. If a woman spent many years serving others as a wife and mother, she can now be self-indulgent at home without feeling guilty or fearing criticism. As the head of her own household, she now makes the decisions about how her time and money will be spent and finds comfort in an autonomous life. Even if there is less money to spend, there is satisfaction in being the decisionmaker. Divorced people may also be less lonely than they were in their incompatible marriages. Instead of depending on a spouse for companionship, they are now motivated to widen their circle of friends.

These successful adaptations do not happen overnight. Even if it is the woman who has sought the divorce, there is usually a period of initial shock followed by a period of stocktaking and reassessment. But the feeling of having done the right thing sees the person through these difficult periods. As one forty-eight-year-old woman divorced for five years put it:

> I knew without a doubt that I had done the right thing. It was as if I'd awakened from a bad dream. It's really not a bad life at all, at least not the way people think it is. In fact, in many ways, I feel as if I escaped from a burning house.[11]

The Widowed at Midlife: Prior to 1900, only 40 percent of women in America got married, had children, launched them into the world, and survived with their husbands into old age. The remaining 60 percent did not reach marriageable age, did not marry, died before childbirth, or were widowed while their children were young. Widowhood was a common experience for those in midlife, but with greater longevity that experience has been pushed into later decades for most people. At present, only one in twenty women aged forty-five to fifty becomes widowed.

The likelihood of a man in this age group becoming a widower is even smaller (one in a hundred)—and these men readily remarry. Widowhood is more common among women than among men because women outlive men, tend to marry men older than themselves, and are less likely to remarry than are widowed men.

Much of the literature on widowhood pertains to women in their sixties or older, so it is not directly applicable to the fifty-year-old woman whose husband dies, although there are a number of common concerns. Furthermore, since many fifty-year-old men and women have widowed mothers, the issue of widowhood concerns many people in midlife.

Younger widows often have a psychologically more difficult task than older ones in adapting to the loss of their husbands. Older women (especially those who have nursed an ailing husband) have some opportunity to "rehearse" for widowhood, and such anticipatory coping makes it easier to deal with death when it comes. Furthermore, because there are many more widows among the older population, it is easier for them to link up with others socially.

A forty-eight-year-old woman whose fifty-year-old husband dies of a heart attack is suddenly faced with an unanticipated life situation. Her children may not yet be entirely on their own, and rarely are they in a position to help her financially. Because a death at this time is perceived as premature, there is a greater sense of loss. But widows in midlife have greater options to reshape their lives than older women, especially if they are not displaced homemakers and have the means to support themselves.

There are important differences between the divorced and the widowed. A widowed woman is less likely to suffer the economic setback of the woman who gets divorced. The loss of future earnings by the husband may be offset by his death benefits and the estate he leaves behind. On the psychological plane, bereavement represents a different emotional burden from the conflict, shame, and anger that often characterize divorce. On the social plane, the death of a spouse rallies friends and relatives to one's side; divorce generates mixed reactions.

A middle-aged or older man who is widowed often faces a period of confusion. The death of his wife represents not only the loss of his primary caretaker, friend, and confidante, but also his main link to friends and relatives. But if his life is firmly anchored in his work, he is less likely to suffer the loss of identity and status experienced by women who are widowed. He may also find himself in high demand if he chooses to remarry, which most widowers do.

The loss of a spouse is a major source of stress. One-fifth of the surviving spouses continue to show signs of depression a year after the death of the husband or wife. For a period of five years following the death of the spouse, the death rates of the surviving partners are higher than would be predicted for their ages. Beyond that period, however, life expectancy for the widowed returns to average rates.[12] With the passage of time, most people who have lost a spouse are psychologically fully reconstituted and show no significant differences from others in mood, sense of self-worth, satisfaction with accomplishments, and sense of integrity.

The Never-Married at Fifty: One out of twenty men and women are still single at fifty and tend to arouse curiosity, concern, and envy, depending on one's own perspective on marriage.

Now that homosexuals are less stigmatized and therefore more willing to reveal themselves, it has become clearer that a substantial proportion of those who never marry, especially if male, belong to this group. But the single man or woman is not necessarily gay. Furthermore, as many more gay couples now live together openly, they are single only in a legal sense.

Never-married women are more likely than wives to have been successful at full-time occupations. Because they are self-supporting, they may have been either more demanding in their marital choices or more threatening to men of traditional orientation. Alternatively, women who are not interested in marriage may pursue higher levels of education to prepare for a career that will enable them to become financially independent. One investigator calls these women the "cream of the crop" in contrast to those middle-aged bachelors who are "the bottom of the barrel"—unable to attract a wife because of being poor providers or unfit in one or another manner.[13] As usual, such designations do not fit every case.

The educational level of singles also confirms this discrepancy. Men with less than five years of schooling and women with more than four years of college are most likely to be single within the population aged thirty-five to fifty-four (which has the highest proportion of married couples). Because a serious lack of education often reflects a mental, physical, or social handicap, it is easy to see why these persons would be less desirable as marital partners. But there are single men who do not fit this image at all. They may be seen as highly desirable mates by women but choose not to settle down for reasons of their own.

Being single is now viewed in a more positive light ("creative singlehood"). And being single does not mean being alone. Like the divorced and widowed, the never-married may have a wide circle of friends and relatives. They may carry on intermittent sexual affairs or remain celibate. On the other hand, the popular image of the "swinging single" life-style is largely a fantasy of those who are not single.

CULTIVATING SINGLEHOOD

Men and women who stay unmarried past age fifty may want this option for a variety of reasons and lead lives that have their own satisfactions and dissatisfactions. Many widows and widowers say they don't intend to marry again because no one could possibly replace the wonderful spouse who has died. While these people emphasize the virtues of the departed, divorced people of both sexes tend to act out their hostilities to former spouses in their subsequent relationships with the opposite sex. In most cases, however, these reactions of both the widowed and the divorced are only temporary. Having been married at one time, these men and women may wish to marry again.

Divorced or widowed women are in a somewhat different situation than men. Their problems of being single at fifty are twofold: real and symbolic. The real problems are a reflection of life circumstances. But the symbolic burden of being single is gratuitous. Many of these women don't need a husband and don't want a husband. What they need is economic, social, and psychological support. By holding the ideal of marriage to be the normative state, society makes single women feel incomplete. They are expected to search constantly for "the right man," even though there is increasingly less likelihood of finding him.

Our culture is so focused on the nuclear family that we tend to see all human interactions in that context, although there are, of course, many fifty-year-olds who in effect do not have families that are close enough to call their own. Yet their need for intimacy is no less, and the importance of cultivating close ties is no less crucial to their middle years and beyond. It has been shown that the presence of an intimate relationship—someone to whom we can reveal our joys and sorrows—is highly important for older people in particular. The presence of such a confidant acts as a buffer against the inevitable hardships we suffer as we grow older (such as loss of status, widowhood, dependency, and ill health). A widow with such ties fares even better than one with a husband who fails to fulfill this role, and the more stable the confidant relationship over the years, the more effective it appears to be.

In a sample of older individuals, 80 percent with a long-term confidant were deemed psychologically "unimpaired," as against 20 percent of those lacking such support. The impaired would, of course,

---

MIDDLE-AGE DATING*
by Noel Perrin

I'm dialing a phone number and when I've touched five digits, I suddenly hang up. For two or three minutes I sit on my bed, my lips moving occasionally, as if I were an actor going over a part. Then I pick up the phone, hesitate, start to put it down again. Instead, I quickly touch seven tones. A woman answers.

I'm a nervous man in his 50's, calling a woman also in her 50's to ask her to dinner. It will be a blind date. It will be my second blind date this month. Dear god, how I dread it.

. . . Those first dates are *hard*. They're not hard to arrange—half my friends know someone I should call. What's hard is the actual evening. There is not going to be that instant and spontaneous attraction that leads to second and third dates when you're young. For the young, sexual attraction serves as a kind of handy glue, keeping a couple together until other and more durable bonds take hold. Shared memories, shared thoughts, perhaps, eventually, shared children.

A little of that glue is still available to people in their 50's (and even older, I hear). In rare cases, quite a lot. More typically, though, a man and woman in their 50's spend the first date making allowances for its absence. They're thinking that if they should come to love each other, her wrinkles or

---

also have a harder time hanging on to a confidant over time. For the unmarried, therefore, the primary search is not necessarily for a spouse but for friends, companionship, and intimacy. For people who have felt isolated in their marriages, new vistas of meaningful relationships open up after the marriage is dissolved.

Dating is primarily a form of exploratory courtship, even if it is not meant to lead to marriage. Dating patterns are shaped by the young. For older actors, there are few scripts. Whether the aim of the encounter is a one-night stand or eventual marriage, the midlife male and female can neither compete effectively nor imitate with ease the

his potbelly would be no barrier. But how do you get from first meeting to love, to what was once called being stuck on someone—with so little glue?

One way is to share some memories before you start. That's why so many people, when they get divorced or widowed, look around to see who they knew in high school that might also be coming back on the market.

Another is to try a different brand of glue. Wealth and fame have served older men quite well for centuries—usually, I grant, to cement relationships with younger women rather than with their contemporaries. They have also served wealthy and famous women. "A duchess is never more than 30 years old to a snob," Stendhal once wrote. But these artificial glues, though handy for some purposes, are flawed. They are not effective in building true intimacy, the only real antidote to loneliness.

True intimacy is the whole purpose of middle-age dating. Only what took one date to accomplish at twenty-five may now take five or ten. By middle age, people have developed complex personalities, whole networks of obligations, settled habits. It would be naive to expect any quick meshing. . . .

But then, we're deeper people now. With luck, we might wind up with the kind of rich and tolerant relationship we didn't even dream of when we were young.

* From "Middle-Age Dating" by Noel Perrin, published in the *New York Times Magazine* July 6, 1968. Copyright 1986 by The New York Times Company. Reprinted by permission.

manners of youth. So they must evolve new dating patterns more suitable to their needs.

As an alternative to singles bars, numerous opportunities are offered by churches, clubs, and various other organizations for mature and unattached men and women to mingle. For people who come together for some meaningful activity—intellectual, artistic, athletic, political—there is a greater likelihood of meeting others who share their interests and of enjoying themselves than at gatherings that are merely thinly veiled attempts at matchmaking.

Professional women in large cities are also seeking novel ways of pooling their resources by offering ex-husbands, ex-boyfriends, colleagues, clients, and any other eligible men they know—and can vouch for as single, successful, and sane—for other women's consideration.[14]

BETWEEN TWO GENERATIONS

In the past, the adult members in a community were typically limited to two generations—young adults and their parents. By contrast there are now adults who belong to three or even four generations—children, parents, grandparents, and great grandparents. One of the consequences of this demographic pattern is that middle-aged individuals find themselves sandwiched between young-adult offspring who are not yet completely self-sufficient and parents who are becoming increasingly less self-sufficient.

Parenting at Midlife: Very few people become parents at fifty; those who do are usually divorced or widowed men who, in their second marriages, have younger wives who want to have children of their own. Otherwise, the children of midlife parents typically range from their late teens to their late twenties. It is not unusual, however, for some parents in midlife to have their youngest child still in high school, and for others to have their oldest out of college and married with young children of their own. The parenting tasks of midlife thus may range from child-rearing to grandparenthood.

Middle-aged parents with teenage children may have a particularly hard time if they resent having to deal with problems of adolescents while others in their age group are enjoying their newly found freedom. On the other hand, older parents of teenagers may enjoy the advantages of greater patience, time, and resources at their disposal.

Having to go through their own midlife transition, they may find it easier to empathize with the growing pains of adolescence.

Parents with college-age children face the standard concerns over the educational and vocational choice their children are making and wonder what kind of life their offspring are leading on their own. Financing of higher education is burdensome at any age, and midlife parents who are already concerned about their postretirement income may find it a serious drain on their resources.

A great deal of concern has been expressed over parental reaction to the "empty nest." As yet there is no substantial evidence that the empty nest constitutes a crisis or even an occasion of significant loss. On the contrary, many parents are delighted at the timely departure of their children. When the children go on to college or to a job, the parents simultaneously gain freedom and independence. Parents who are fond of their children miss them when they are away, but only those whose sense of worth is solely and inextricably tied up with their parental role are likely to have serious problems.

The empty nest situation changes abruptly when older, sometimes married, children come back home to live with their parents while struggling to find adequate jobs. Graduation from college, therefore, does not by any means signify the end of parental responsibilities for the support of children.

As sons and daughters become adults, their relationship with their parents undergoes distinct changes, and children become an increasingly important source of influence on their parents. Mothers, in particular, report that their children's encouragement is an important factor in their returning to work or going back to school. Fathers are more influenced by their children's views on current issues. Through their children, many middle-aged parents keep in touch with new trends and developments in the culture.

Grandparenthood: Grandparenthood is no longer the exclusive province of the elderly; many people (more often women) in their early fifties now have grandchildren. Some young grandparents are delighted to welcome a new generation in the family. But for those who dread the thought of getting old, the appearance of a grandchild may force them prematurely into a role they typically associate with the elderly.

More generally, two styles of grandparenting have been described. One is a fun-seeking relationship, the other a more distant manner of relating to the grandchild.[15] Young grandparents are more likely to join the child in various activities for the express purpose of having fun. Because they are not directly responsible for the child's upbringing, they can be quite indulgent with their grandchildren, leaving to the parents the job of setting limits and other less pleasant tasks of socialization, although the older generation can also help to inculcate traditional values.

Those who have a more distant relationship usually see their grandchildren on special holidays like Thanksgiving. Limiting interaction to these family occasions tends to make them less personal, and children see their grandparents as distant but benevolent figures.

There are more grandmothers than grandfathers, and women tend to be more involved than men in the lives of their children's families. Grandmothers may welcome their new role or resent being drawn back into child-rearing responsibilities. Conflicts over the values and life-styles of teenage grandchildren are another source of grief.

Relationships with Parents: Those who have had smooth relationships with their parents find in midlife that their mutual and close affections take on greater depth, tinged with a bittersweet element as parents approach the end of their lives. If there has been conflict, this period provides an opportunity to bury the hatchet and try to make up for past hurts on either side.

There is no evidence that families are now more alienated from their elderly than they were in the past or that parents are being abandoned to institutions or to their own fate. Actually, no more than 5 percent of the elderly are cared for in institutions such as nursing homes, and strenuous efforts are made by most families to care for the physical and psychological needs of their parents in home settings. However, the proportion of institutionalized elderly rises sharply with age from 2 percent for those sixty-five to seventy-five to over 19 percent for those eighty-five and over, as older people become less able to fend for themselves. Wherever they may be living, about a third of the elderly need supportive services from others.

The burden of such support is more often borne by daughters than by sons, particuarly when everyday assistance and contact are necessary. When these "women in the middle" must contend not only with the needs of parents but sometimes with the needs of grandparents as well, the empty nest is more than offset by a new set of responsibilities, this time to one's family of origin. Women who are trying to start or refashion careers in midlife must balance these responsibilities with this new extension of family obligations.

In assisting their elderly parents, daughters (and sometimes daughters-in-law) will shop and run errands; provide personal care; perform household maintenance tasks; mobilize, coordinate and monitor services from other sources; and fill in when an arranged care program breaks down.[16] There are also sons who take on the major responsibility for the care of their parents. But more typically they help with financial arrangements and become primarily involved during times of major crises.

Illness is the heaviest and most common burden for old parents and their children. The average cost of caring for patients aged sixty-five and over, during the year that they die in a hospital, is $14,000; the overall cost of care during the same year is closer to $30,000.[17] In the absence of adequate insurance and other resources, the cost of caring for elderly parents can place an enormous drain on their middle-aged children, who themselves are beginning to eye their post-retirement life with some apprehension.

No less taxing is the psychological toll of helping parents endure incapacitating chronic ailments or seeing them through their terminal illness. There is no easy way of dealing with these problems, but whether they become embittering burdens or deeply meaningful experiences partly depends on you.

To attend to endless practical problems, to provide compassion and companionship, and to work through your own feelings, you need time. You must marshal psychological resources, both to help the dying depart in peace and dignity and to deal with the mixed emotions of sadness and relief that will follow your parents' death. It is your last chance to fulfill a role that is going to be lost to you forever. Apart from the pain and anguish, the mundane and the practical, you must find some way to give meaning to your interactions with your parents.

The writing of this book coincided with the terminal illness of my ninety-two-year-old mother. Simultaneously, I worked on the translation of her autobiography, the account of an extraordinary life written by a remarkable woman. We labored together, using every moment at our disposal—in the hospital, waiting in clinics and corridors, at home, and on our ever shorter walks. Through the etchings of time on her face and in her luminous eyes, I saw the child of a past century come alive, the sparkle of a lovely woman shine through, and the grace of a generous soul live on.

6

CAREER
AND
CREATIVITY

E

The adage that the middle years are a time to reap is more valid with respect to career and achievement than to any other aspect of life. Having invested in the future by preparing for it during youth, and having toiled away at our work during young adulthood, we are ready at midlife to gather in full measure the fruits of our labors.

At fifty most American professionals, executives, people who own their own businesses, and skilled technicians are as well established in their careers as they are ever likely to be. Their earnings have peaked, and they have built a substantial equity to sustain them in their declining years. Having attained ample altitude, most careers coast along nicely in the fifties.

This pattern holds true for many but by no means for all. For those who are destined to reach the top, this is the time when careers begin to soar. Others begin to lose altitude and face the distressing prospect that obsolescence or a disastrous crash may end their vocational lives prematurely.

Women who have spent their time primarily keeping house and raising families face a variety of prospects. With her children on their own, a midlife woman may devote her newly found freedom and extra time to the pursuit of personal interests, volunteer work, or simply settling down to a more leisurely life. Those with stalled careers may turn their full energies to reviving them. Yet others go back to school, acquire new skills, and launch themselves into the workplace.

For each of these groups of men and women, career success and satisfaction are likely to have different meanings.

THE MEANING OF WORK

Work is by no means an isolated stream in our lives. Every issue we have discussed so far is intimately linked with work. The work we do has significant impact on our health, our personalities, and our relationships with our families.

Those who make up the great majority of the world's population work in order to provide for the basic necessities of life. But for those who are more fortunate, work is expected to provide far more than a means of survival. We expect physical comfort and a few luxuries as a reward for our labors. We aspire to attain and maintain social status through our careers. We seek a purpose in life through what we do for ourselves or through serving others. We yearn for creativity—some distinctive, if not unique, contribution that will outlive us and lend our names and memories a measure of immortality.

The Value of Work: Work is evaluated by a number of criteria. Its rewards may be extrinsic or intrinsic, altruistic or self-serving. Virtually all occupations fulfill a combination of these aims, although one aim may be more significant than others in any given case.

In free-market societies, the most obvious *extrinsic* reward for work is money. Money buys things and provides security. It also confers power, status, and professional recognition. The *intrinsic* rewards of a job are related to those satisfactions that are independent of its extrinsic rewards. The degree of satisfaction a person obtains from work is in turn a function of both skill and interest. We enjoy what we do well and do better at tasks we find interesting. These two factors, of course, do not always go together, but the presence of one significantly compensates for the absence of the other.

The extrinsic and intrinsic rewards of work cannot be strictly separated in practical terms. Activities rich in extrinsic rewards are also more likely to be perceived as intrinsically interesting. Conversely, the higher the intrinsic rewards the better is the quality of one's work, which usually leads to greater extrinsic rewards. When these two sets of satisfactions do not go together, the discrepancies between extrinsic and intrinsic rewards often cause vocational doubts and crises, especially in midlife.

Economists assume that people are motivated primarily by self-interest and that they are rational in their choices in the sense that they will behave in ways that appear most likely to advance their self-interest: If two identical products are priced differently, one buys the cheaper one. But altruism also constitutes a significant incentive. The opportunity to help others in some tangible way is an important consideration for those who willingly go into service related professions.

Those who succeed in their work are likely to be sustained by external rewards even if they begin to develop doubts about the value of what they do, feel burned out, or merely become bored. But at midlife, the lack of intrinsic satisfaction will erode one's career attachment, and the need for steady and sustained effort will prove increasingly burdensome.

At the more basic level, whether or not you work makes a difference to your sense of self. Holding a job, whatever it may be, not only insures a source of income, but positions you in a meaningful social role. Because you do something, you make a difference; you may not be indispensable, but your failure to perform will have an impact on those who rely on your services, whether you are a bus driver, bank teller, or company president.

At any given time, some 5 to 10 percent of the adult population in the industrial world are out of work. The expectation that all of us will sometime want to or be forced to retire makes the issue of unemployment especially pertinent when we enter the final phase of our active working lives.

The choice of a career, like the choice of a spouse, is crucial, but in itself neither guarantees success nor dooms the outcome. In traditional societies individuals exercised relatively little personal choice in selecting either a spouse or a vocation. We are now far more free to choose in each area, but not as autonomous as we may imagine ourselves to be. Just as the principle of homogamy (mating like with like) governs the choice of a mate, our social background, gender, and life circumstances exert enormous influence on the choice and progress of our careers.

Career choices are influenced by personality characteristics, and the nature of one's work in turn influences one's personality. The molding of a personality through the work experience spills over into other aspects of life. There is a reciprocal relationship between the substantive complexity of a job and the intellectual flexibility of the individual holding the job. Those engaged in intellectually complex work come to exercise their mental prowess not only on the job but also in their nonoccupational lives by becoming more open to new experiences and prone to self-direction. Even their leisure-time activities tend to be more intellectually demanding.[1]

CAREER CONSIDERATIONS
AT MIDLIFE

The physical condition of one's body and the state of one's health are likely to have a major impact on job options and prospects in midlife. One of the consistent changes brought about by aging is the reduction in nerve conduction velocity, or the speed with which impulses travel along nerve fibers. The time it takes to carry out movements increases steadily, so that the rate at which skilled tasks can be performed is reduced. This has important occupational consequences for certain factory workers.

Workers in their forties usually manage to maintain an adequate pace at work because of their experience as well as their willingness to exert more effort. But as they near fifty, those who work at time-stressed jobs, such as piecework on an assembly line, find it increasingly difficult to keep up with younger workers. At jobs where speed is a factor this occurs earlier than in more strenuous physical labor that is not time-dependent. Men can go on digging ditches, for example, until their late fifties or early sixties. Thus, when blue-collar workers change jobs because of advancing age, they are likely to shift from less strenuous piecework to heavier manual work, paradoxical as this may sound.

Changes in mental function and personality also influence vocational behavior in midlife. The more sophisticated the job, the less likely people are to switch in or out of it in midlife. This tendency may reflect either a greater degree of job satisfaction or fewer available options.

Family relationships, too, have a close association with career considerations. If your children have left home, your parents are not dependent on you, and you have built up a substantial equity for your older years, the incentive to exert yourself purely for the sake of making more money is weaker. Changed family circumstances are especially influential in the vocational choices of women.

Career status in turn influences family issues. Many midlife men who find their careers stabilized or stalled turn to their families as a source of satisfaction. Others, frustrated at being stuck in their careers, change their family circumstances to start anew on the personal front.

Whether one's career prospects improve, remain steady, or decline influences an individual's self-esteem. Some people enjoy the feeling of having finally arrived at the peak and develop a satisfying sense of gradual closure. Others experience the frustration of not having reached their goals, the realization that their remaining choices are limited, or the anxieties of an uncertain future.

Career Satisfaction.: Vocational competence and satisfaction typically become stabilized in midlife at more or less a peak level. During this period, doctors, lawyers, engineers, accountants, other professionals and executives, and business owners reap the benefits of accumulated years of experience, established contacts, and the momentum they

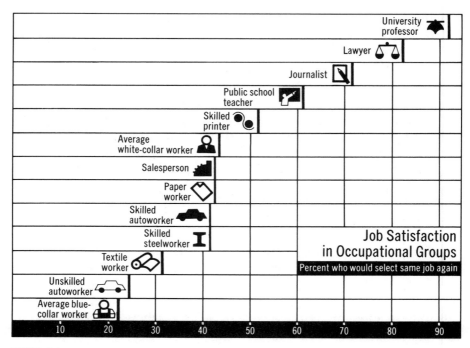

FIGURE 6-1.

have built into their jobs over the decades. In organizational settings, these are the individuals who constitute the backbone of the institutions they serve and are basically responsible for running them.

Surveys of job satisfaction show a rather disheartening picture: Only half the respondents report themselves really satisfied with their jobs. The other half would prefer to have another job (see Figure 6-1). However, a close look at particular occupations reveals a wide discrepancy in levels of job satisfaction. More than 90 percent of university professors but only 20 percent of blue-collar workers are very satisfied with their jobs. Generally, the professions lead the field in level of satisfaction, followed by white-collar and blue-collar workers. Income is obviously an important consideration but not the only one. Public school teachers show considerably higher levels of satisfaction than some areas of work that pay higher wages.

In the majority of middle-class occupations, midlife brings neither a marked decline nor a sharp rise in career prospects. For most of us, the careers we maintain in midlife are neither unmitigated successes nor disasters. Rather, they are mixed blessings on which we must continue to depend for financial sustenance and psychological satisfaction.

The feeling of being in charge was clearly in evidence among the middle-aged male business executives studied by Bernice Neugarten and her associates. These men showed a sense of mastery, competence, and control. Their successful performance over the years had made them confident of their highly developed ability to make decisions and to manage a complex environment. They had a clear sense of who they were and had no wish to change places with their younger selves. As one man put it:

> I know now exactly what I can do best, and how to make the best use of my time. . . . I know how to delegate authority, but also what decisions to make myself. . . . I know how to buffer myself from troublesome people. . . . One well-placed telephone call will get me what I need. It takes time to learn how to cut through the red tape and how to get the organization to work for me. . . . All this is what makes the difference between me and a young man, and it's all this that gives me the advantage.[2]

From such secure platforms, some men and women take off on their final trajectory to positions of leadership in the top echelons of organizational hierarchies to become the chief executives, directors, and other senior officers in various businesses. In other institutional settings, a college professor becomes a university president, or a lawyer or business executive is appointed to high government office. The sense of accomplishment perceived by the individual is relative. One person may be bitterly disappointed at not making it beyond the vice-presidency of a company, while another, many rungs lower in the hierarchy, is delighted by a promotion to supervisor.

Midlife is by no means the last chance for reaching the pinnacle of one's career. But those who attain the high points of their careers in their sixties or even later tend to be the exceptions. And unless the basic ingredients for ultimate advancement are already present at fifty, there is little likelihood of any dramatic shift in career prospects later on.

Those who have reached the peak of their aspirations can now fly high above the clouds, stable and on course. They are in the enviable position of sustaining a life of action while simultaneously generating opportunities for a life of contemplation. This is the time to go beyond technical managerial competence, to begin to acquire the wider perspective and the greater depth of the elder statesman. It is also a time to enjoy the financial rewards of your labors and to share them with those persons and causes that mean most to you.

Some midlife careers are ostensibly successful when they have in effect stalled: professionals who fail to keep up with the advances in their fields yet manage to retain their status; scholars who continue to publish but have little new to say; executives who still run the show but have lost initiative. As Roger Bacon noted astutely back in the thirteenth century, "Men of age object too much, consult too long, adventure too little, repent too soon, and seldom drive business home to the full period, but content themselves with a mediocrity of success."

Loss of Employment: The feeling that one has not accomplished enough in life or that one has chosen the wrong line of work are among the particular career concerns of middle age. More immediate and more serious are the problems that confront those with minimal skills and erratic work patterns, who are likely to find it increasingly difficult to sustain themselves. Because the performance of unskilled tasks does not keep on improving with experience, many middle-aged workers cannot claim greater expertise. Rapid shifts in technology will doom some to obsolescence no matter how good they are at their jobs. And forces totally outside one's control, such as the state of the economy, may lead to layoffs, with meager prospects of being rehired. Unscrupulous employers may also replace senior employees with less expensive younger workers.

The reaction to prolonged joblessness among middle-class professionals follows a distinctive pattern. The initial impact is typically one of disbelief, shock, frustration, and anger. This stage is followed by a period of temporary relief, even a certain sense of relaxation and enjoyment of newfound freedom and greater involvement with one's family. For a while, the person is sustained by the hope of finding another job. But if casual and then concerted efforts to find work repeatedly fail, vacillation and doubt set in and may eventually lead to the hopelessness and cynicism of the permanently unemployed.[3]

Even without such dramatic setbacks, many middle-aged men and women find their careers losing momentum. The sense of stagnation, of being burned out or drained, of having been used and pushed aside are embittering. The anger that such feelings generate cannot even be openly expressed for fear of making a bad situation worse.

Those who continue to do the job ostensibly as before may also harbor a gnawing feeling that they no longer measure up to their colleagues or to their own expectations. The prospect of becoming "deadwood" is galling even if the security of one's job is not at stake. Yet circumstances are seldom so bleak that people cannot get back on their feet even though the work they manage to find may be a far cry from what they want or deserve. Despite the severity of the financial hardship that befalls these individuals, the blow to their self-esteem may be greatly mitigated by the realization that the value of who one is does not depend solely on what one does to earn a living.

In the light of these concerns, midlife career changes and early retirement have become topics of increasing interest to the middle-aged population. Because of the optimism that pervades current attitudes toward aging, there is, at times, a tendency to romanticize the prospects. Whether people are forced to make choices, or are in the enviable position of having options, they need a realistic approach as much as they need a cheerful attitude before taking the plunge.

CAREER CHANGE

Shifts in careers and work patterns in midlife may be voluntary or may be imposed upon the individual. The forty-eight-year-old executive whose company has collapsed, leaving him with no immediate job prospects, the fifty-two-year-old dentist who has sold his practice and is looking for ways to invest his substantial assets, the forty-nine-year-old mother of two adult children who has gone back to school to become an accountant—all these represent very different forms of career change at midlife.

There is nothing unusual about people changing jobs and careers. Almost a third of all workers transfer to different occupations over a period of five years.[4] Among men such shifts are most common between the ages of sixteen and nineteen (over half of this group switch jobs) and only half as likely to occur among those fifty to fifty-nine. Among women, the age discrepancy is more modest: 38 percent of those sixteen to nineteen, compared to 25 percent of those in their fifties, switch occupations.

The likelihood of shifts among various occupations differs widely according to vocation. Nonfarm workers are more than twice as likely as farmers to change vocations. Professional and technical workers are least likely to transfer to different occupations: 63 percent of the men and 55 percent of the women in this group remain employed in the same occupation over a five-year period. In the professional and technical occupations, physicians, dentists, lawyers, and judges are most stable in their career; more than 80 percent remain in the same occupation. The least stable groups include female recreation workers and male elementary school teachers. Among men in their fifties, professionals, craftsmen, and farmers are least likely to change occupations; among women, professionals, those working in sales, and those employed in private households show the highest vocational stability.

Occupational mobility continues into midlife, but both the propensity to change jobs and the opportunities for doing so decline sharply with age. In one study, the average rate of employed people moving into new occupations was 37 percent for those eighteen to nineteen and 4 percent for those forty-five to fifty-four.[5]

Many studies show that because the shifts tend to be relatively minor, the move from one line of work to another does not radically alter the worker's life circumstances. More significant changes can be subsumed under career advancement, when the motivation underlying such moves is not discontent but the challenges and benefits of the new opportunity. Lawyers shifting from the private to the public sector, academicians taking administrative roles, engineers moving into management—all these exemplify such shifts.

Radical career change, on the other hand, entails a drastic break motivated by intense career dissatisfaction. Most midlife men and women who feel trapped in their work look for sources of satisfaction in other areas of their lives—family, friends, hobbies, travel, sports, intellectual and aesthetic pursuits. Only a few of the more seriously discontented make a clean break by moving away from the community and starting on a wholly new style of life and work; and those who do so are more likely to be in their early forties than in their fifties.[6]

Whether you chose the wrong career or merely became disenchanted with it, a realistic assessment is of the first importance in trying to decide where to go from here. Because of the parallel between career selection and the choice of a mate, between the evolution over time of a marriage and that of a career, a similar set of questions arises at midlife: Is this what I want? Is this the best I can do? The fact that another person is at stake in a marriage but usually not in a job situation is, of course, a significant consideration. But if the change in career is not externally imposed by the loss of one's job, or the work situation is not intolerable, how does one decide if and when to make a career shift? In the cold light of reason, what exactly are one's options?

Unless there are compelling circumstances, it makes little sense for a middle-aged individual to abandon a long-standing career. If your work has gone stale, you may be tempted to look for greener pastures. But if your workplace is not intolerable and the sources of your dissatisfaction are rather nebulous, think twice before taking a leap into the void. Be especially careful not to depreciate the value of what you have or allow the promises of possible alternatives to appear rosier than warranted. In careers as in marriages, if you apply the same levels of thought and energy that you would be willing to invest in a novel prospect, it is often easier to fix an existing situation than to start all over again in midlife.

Once you give up your unfulfilled and unrealistic expectations, your career may start trotting like an unburdened mule. By concentrating on what you like to do and what you do well at your job, you will markedly increase your satisfaction. By finding your niche on the side of the hill, you may even be glad to be spared the rigors of standing in the wind on top of the mountain.

Some people have certainly made spectacular escapes from a humdrum existence at midlife by either changing careers or choosing early retirement. But making it work takes a special type of person, sizable assets, and a willingness to take a chance.

At age fifty, as you look to the years ahead, think about how your life is likely to appear from the perspective of age sixty, seventy, and beyond. Then live your life in ways that will provide you with contentment, not regret. Remember that by not doing the right thing, you cause yourself as much grief as by doing the wrong thing.

Early Retirement: Retirement suggests a shift from full-time, year-round, gainful employment to a life sustained mainly by financial resources other than current earnings. This general pattern, however, subsumes a variety of alternatives. At one extreme is the person who has completely and permanently withdrawn from the labor force; at the other extreme is the fully pensioned military officer who has started on a second full-time career.

Most people in midlife are actively engaged in the work force. In the forty-five-to-fifty-four-year-old group, 91 percent of the men and 63 percent of the women were employed in 1984. (Men and women in this age category account for 15 percent of the civilian labor force.)[7]

These percentages are only slightly lower than the peak employment rates, which for men are about 95 percent of the twenty-five-to-forty-four-year-old group and for women about 70 percent of the twenty-to-forty-four-year old group.

Retirement is considered "early" if it occurs before the mandatory age. It has become increasingly common in recent years for those in their late fifties and early sixties to withdraw from active employment before they have to. Over the quarter of a century following World War II, the proportion of men fifty-five to sixty-four in the labor force declined from 89.6 to 80.5 percent. The decline was particularly steep after 1970.

Although poor health is often cited as the reason for early retirement, there is no evidence that older men are now more apt to suffer illness than they were in 1946. Changes in Social Security retirement and disability benefits are more likely explanations. Since 1961 workers have had the option of collecting benefits at age sixty-two, and benefit levels have been rising faster than the cost of living. There has been an eightfold increase in the aggregate payments of Social Security disability benefits between 1965 and 1978, mainly because many low-wage earners have availed themselves of these government-financed alternatives to work.[8]

Retirement options generally do not extend to those in their early fifties. Furthermore, even those who could afford to retire at this time are unlikely to do so for a variety of social and psychological reasons. Unless there is a compelling reason for a man to stop working early, most people see such a move as unnatural or self-indulgent. As a result, only about 5 percent of men in their fifties can be expected to retire early, compared to 20 percent of those in their early sixties. A higher percentage express an intention to retire early, but as the reality of such a decision becomes more imminent, they change their minds —either because the economic feasibility of retiring early becomes more problematic, or because the prospect of retiring becomes less attractive for other reasons. Hence most fifty-year-olds face at least another decade of full employment and need to make the most of it.

Working women share many of the concerns of men with respect to early retirement. But in the case of married women, an important additional incentive to retire early is the retirement of the husband, who is usually older and retiring on schedule. The working wife may want to stop working because of the possibility of relocating to some other part of the country, for more leisure, or to keep the retired husband company.

It is generally assumed that retirement is less of a problem for married women because they usually invest fewer years in their jobs and can more readily fall back on their domestic role when they leave the labor market. But, in fact, middle-class women who have a serious interest in their work have more, not less, difficulty than men in adjusting to retirement. Retired women are reported to be more often lonely, anxious, depressed, or low in self-esteem and stability.[9] Apart from psychological considerations, women have greater reason to be concerned about their financial future. Older women in America constitute the single poorest group in the country. Half of those over sixty-five live at or below poverty level.

Women and Work: Enormous changes have occurred over the past several decades in the vocational attitudes and behavior of women. The most dramatic shift perhaps is in the sheer number of women who have joined the work force. Since the mid-1950s, there has been a steady influx of white women into the labor force. As shown in Figure 6-2, white women constitute the only group to show such a trend; the rates of employment of black women have remained fairly steady. The participation rate of white working women in their mid-fifties to mid-sixties made its sharpest gains before 1970, when it stabilized at a level somewhat lower than that of black women and much lower than that of men. Women accounted for 27 percent of the civilian work force in 1940 and 55 percent in 1985.

In 1985, the proportion of women forty-five to sixty-four who were working was 51 percent for the married, 73 percent for the never-married, and 61 percent for the widowed, divorced, and separated. The greatest increase has been in the married group, among whom only 34 percent were working outside the home in 1960; the rates for the other groups have not changed that much. (The rate for widowed, divorced, and separated women has gone up by 2 percentage points; the rate for the never-married has declined to the same degree.)

The vocational patterns of never-married women are closest to those of men. They work for the same reasons that men do, and when they are not handicapped by sex discrimination, their careers progress along the same paths as those of their male counterparts. Unmarried women who have worked full-time throughout adulthood face the same set of assets and liabilities as men do at midlife. A never-married woman can give her undivided attention to her career because she

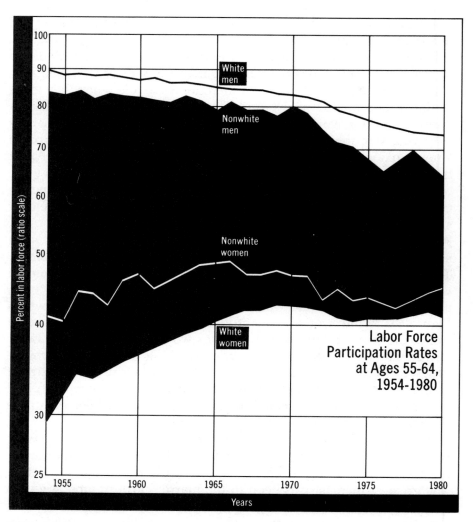

FIGURE 6-2.

has no spouse and children to consider. But so far as parents are concerned, a woman's obligations are likely to be no less than a man's.

The circumstances at midlife of widowed and divorced working women depends in part on how old they were when their marriages ended and whether they have worked since then. A woman who got divorced at thirty-five, went to work or back to school, and was established in a career by the time she was forty may be no more disadvantaged than her single counterpart if she has no children to rear and support.

The proportion of never-married women who work has not changed over the past four decades, because the need to make a living is the primary incentive for these women (and most men) to work. In fact, 75 percent of working women are either single mothers or married to men earning less than $15,000 a year.[10] When a job and extra income are not essential, married women are likely to have other incentives to work, such as intellectual interests and the need for self-fulfillment.

Whatever her marital status, a midlife woman who wants to enter the job market faces considerable difficulty. Especially hard pressed are the displaced homemakers with modest educational backgrounds and few marketable skills. The jobs that are generally available to them tend to be uninteresting, unfulfilling, and poorly paid. Only a few get on a career track leading to advancement, status, adequate remuneration, and job satisfaction.

Despite large gains in employment figures, women still make only sixty cents for every dollar earned by men. Women of forty-five to fifty-four earn 54 percent of the amount earned by their male counterparts. Several variables account for this discrepancy. Women now in their middle years are not on the average as well educated as men of their age. This generation of women were socialized into primarily homemaker roles. Many have had extended nonworking periods when they interrupted their careers to raise children. Finally, midlife women, more than younger women, are likely to encounter employer bias.

Forty-eight percent of women over forty-five work in the area of retail sales, unskilled or semiskilled factory work, private household work, and similar service jobs. Another 28 percent are employed in clerical work.[11] Women still account for 99 percent of secretaries, 96 percent of nurses, 90 percent of bookkeepers, and 88 percent of those who wait table. But women do not have all of the menial and low-paying jobs: They account for only 23 percent of janitors and cleaners and 10 percent of laborers.

In spite of these grim realities, the world is changing. Bank tellers, insurance adjusters, and real estate agents—all formerly male-dominated occupations—are now predominantly female. Women also accounted for 27 percent of managers in 1980 as against 15 percent in 1970. Some six million women now earn higher incomes than their husbands.[12] More important, women now constitute a higher proportion than ever before of the students in some of the most prestigious medical, law, and business schools.

These trends may be happening too late to help most midlife women. But statistics apply to groups, not to every individual within a group. Many women in midlife have made spectacular shifts in their careers.

Married women who choose not to work outside the home in midlife give a variety of reasons for their choice. They obtain their satisfactions from their families and from volunteer work and may have no need for an independent income. Should one's husband die, the income from Social Security, private pensions, life insurance benefits, and the husband's estate might be quite adequate for a comfortable life. These women do not have a compelling need for self-fulfillment through a job. Quite content with what they have accomplished and who they are, they intend to carry on without any major shifts in midlife or later.

INCOME

Income typically varies over the life cycle; it rises gradually during young adulthood, reaches a peak in midlife, and declines when the person retires from the labor force.

Most workers have a period of postschool training during which they prepare for a job. Because an apprenticeship maximizes the opportunities for future income, the worker accepts lower wages as an apprentice than he or she might earn at other work. At one extreme is the lengthy education and training of physicians—it takes up to fifteen years following high school to become qualified as a surgical specialist. At the other extreme is the brief on-the-job training that most unskilled workers receive.

Education confers definite advantages. Although the career curve of professionals flattens out at age fifty, earnings generally increase with age in proportion to the time invested in education and the postschool investment in human capital. Thus, the earnings of physicians at ages fifty-five to sixty-five are 2.4 times their income at ages twenty-five to thirty-four; for lawyers and judges, 1.95 times; for engineers, 1.26 times. Clerical workers register a slighter gain (1.11), while retail clerks and truck drivers lose some ground (.98 and .95 times their earlier earnings). There are income inequities at all ages, but they become more pronounced between the ages of forty and sixty, not only because of widening differences in wage rates but also because the better educated withdraw from the labor force later in life.[13]

In midlife, the poor are likely to get poorer, the rich richer; but many middle-class individuals find themselves financially stable, especially if the home mortgage is paid off, and there are sizable assets in retirement plans and other investments. But not everyone enjoys such financial security. Many people live without much thought for the future or without enough money to invest. Their resources may have been depleted by broken marriages, dependent children, or ailing parents.

Even under the best of circumstances, most people in their fifties face decades of life during which their income will inevitably shrink. As illustrated in Figure 6-3, the postretirement years replicate in some ways the days of your youth, except that there are now no parents to take care of you (and you are lucky if you don't have to take care of them). Both youth and old age are characterized by "dissaving," because income is generally less than consumption. For those who are skillful at managing their money, income exceeds consumption during most of adult life (and not just middle age). The central economic task of midlife is to ensure that the disposable income one will need following retirement will be there when the time comes.

The problem of providing for a life span that will typically outlast one's working years is the key financial issue facing the fifty-year-old looking ahead. For the average worker in midlife, income does not fall, but its rate of increase diminishes in inflation-adjusted terms. From the early thirties to the fifties, there is a 9 percent gain in income—and a doubling of real income in less than eight years; in the decade of the fifties, real income rises at 2 percent, and it takes thirty years to double.[14]

As a fifty-year-old, you will not necessarily be facing a losing game, but you must be prepared to live with a zero-sum game. Since your real purchasing power is not likely to grow significantly, any extra expenditure will have to be accompanied by a reduction of some current expenditure. Setting extras aside, the key concern is to make certain that you will have enough capital to live on comfortably beyond retirement, with adequate cushioning against unforeseen circumstances such as chronic illness.

When the fifty-year-old looks at the future, the primary financial considerations should be safety and security. Although there is always

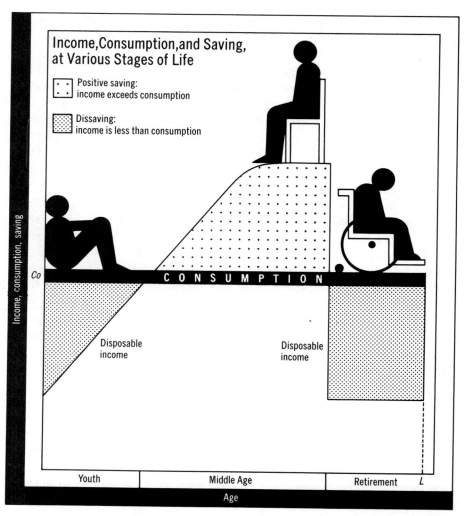

FIGURE 6-3.

the hope of an upturn in fortunes, most men and women over fifty must be concerned with retaining economic altitude—or losing it as slowly as possible. It is foolish to throw caution to the winds by gambling away your hard-earned reserves on the premise that this is your last chance to strike it rich. If you are not rich by now, there is little likelihood of your becoming rich hereafter. But it is equally foolish to be relentlessly nagged by the prospect of strained circumstances in old age and to fret away the remaining years of your life preparing for misfortunes that may never come, instead of enjoying the fruits of your labors. The only thing you cannot afford to do is fail to plan ahead.

CREATIVITY AND CAREER ACCOMPLISHMENT

Those who take the provision of life's necessities for granted search for additional meaning and significance when pondering the success of their careers at midlife. These assessments are typically cast in terms of how productive, creative, and useful one's work has been and how permanent a legacy of accomplishment one is likely to leave behind. Another criterion is how much sheer enjoyment one has derived from work—how much fun has it been?

These issues are difficult to assess either subjectively or objectively. Satisfaction over one's accomplishments is largely relative to one's own expectations and subject to comparison with the work of others. Objective measures of accomplishment are equally difficult. Peer judgments, which often constitute the crucial test of the value of one's work, are far from immutable or infallible. Only the test of time will show whose work proves to be enduring. The very definition of creativity itself is problematic, as the term is applied to everything from designing skyscrapers to the shaping of sand castles at the seashore.

These uncertainties notwithstanding, some interesting attempts have been made at correlating creative achievements with age. Harvey Lehman did an exhaustive study across a wide spectrum of fields (see Figure 6-4). Though creative output is not restricted to any given life period, major creative achievements are clustered relatively early in life—typically around the thirties. Although the study showed that creative individuals continued to be productive, their later work was generally considered less significant than their earlier accomplishments.[15]

In another attempt to study this issue, Wayne Dennis examined the productivity of 738 scholars, scientists, and artists who had lived to at least the age of seventy-nine and found that creative productivity in the older decades varies by field (see Figure 6-5).[16] The work of scholars in the humanities (such as historians and philosophers) remains steadily productive into the seventies; the work of scientists begins to decline slightly in their forties and more markedly after

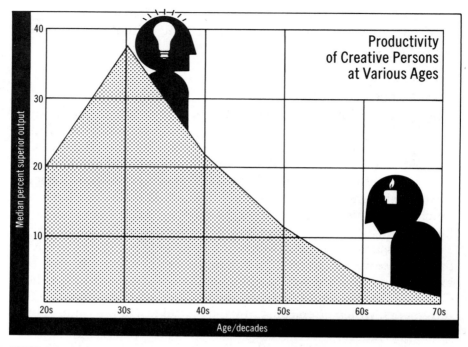

FIGURE 6-4. The curve represents estimates of high quality work in various fields.

their sixties. Those in the arts (like musicians and novelists) reach a creative peak in their forties and become progressively less productive thereafter.

Such attempts at qualifying creativity may be viewed with skepticism because their findings are obviously highly dependent on particular historical and cultural settings. Moreover, even if such statements about midlife are valid in the aggregate, they do not apply to every individual within the group. Thus, even if the productive output of most artists declines in their older years, Pablo Picasso, Pablo Casals, Vladimir Horowitz, and many others have remained dominant figures in their fields into their seventies and beyond.

For the majority of us who cannot aspire to such eminence at any age, the broader issue to be considered at midlife is that of generativity as Erikson defines it. Creativity and career accomplishments are not the only components of the generative process. Lofty concerns about what will remain of value down through the centuries need worry very few of us. We can use other more modest and more personal means to assess the significance of our accomplishments. Individuals

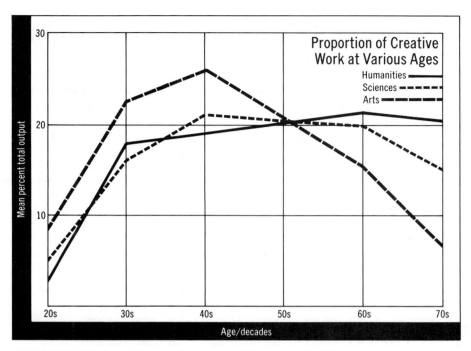

FIGURE 6-5. Each of the three areas is represented by several disciplines.

in midlife can experience a full sense of career accomplishment in a job well done and in fulfilling the all-important task of being mentors to the younger generation. There is certainly a special sense of pride in leaving behind clearly delineated accomplishments that bear one's name. But in an increasingly complex world, a more realistic aim ought to be the satisfaction of having been part of a larger effort, one of the runners of a relay race successfully completed.

THE ACTIVE LIFE AND
THE CONTEMPLATIVE LIFE

We are now approaching the end of this brief excursion into the meaning of being fifty—the high point of mid-life—faced with the prospect of having too much time to do little but not enough time to do much. Each of us needs to determine what he or she will do with the time at hand?

This is not a question to be asked and answered once and for all at fifty but one that needs to be addressed at every major turn in life. Some of the answers will change as you progress from one stage to another, but if there is to be coherence and meaning to your life, some consistency in the answers must run through all the stages.

One of the basic issues that has confronted thoughtful men and women is the choice between a life of action and a life of contemplation. This conflict, first made explicit in the Western cultural tradition in the work of Plato, is not an issue to engage only philosophers and kings but a matter of concern to everyone with a measure of choice in life.[17] Every college student faced with having to choose a career

---

CULTURED RETIREMENT IN THE ANCIENT WORLD

In the Roman world, the ruling class had a long-established tradition whereby as a man retired from the cares of a public career, and, while he still had his wits about him, he entered upon a life of creative leisure at a country estate such as Cicero's beloved villa at Tusculum, in the vicinity of Rome.

This ancient ideal of *otium liberale* ("cultured retirement") appealed greatly to St. Augustine. Before his conversion he planned to marry a rich and well-educated heiress and, after a spell of public life, retire gracefully; yet it turned out otherwise.* His subsequent thoughts on the necessity of combining a life of action and contemplation for a true Christian existence are expressed in the following passage from the *City of God*:**

> As for the three kinds of life, the life of leisure, the life of action, and the combination of the two, anyone, to be sure, might spend his life in any of these ways without detriment to his faith, and might thus attain to the everlasting rewards. What does matter is the answers to those questions: What does a man possess as a result of his love of truth? And what does he pay out in response to the obligations of Christian love? For no one ought to be so leisured as to take no thought in that leisure for the interest of his neighbour, nor so

struggles with this choice even though the issue may not be phrased in just those terms.

When at fifty you are thinking ahead about your work, your family, and the rest of your life, you too are confronting these same choices. For instance, when you plan to retire early, you are in effect opting for a life with a lesser measure of "action" and a greater measure of "contemplation"—which may range from relaxing at a poolside to activities that enrich your mind and spirit.

active as to feel no need for the contemplation of God. The attraction of a life of leisure ought not to be the prospect of lazy inactivity, but the chance for the investigation and discovery of truth, on the understanding that each person makes some progress in this, and does not grudgingly withhold his discoveries from another.

In the life of action, on the other hand, what is to be treasured is not a place of honour or power in this life, since "everything under the sun is vanity" but the task itself that is achieved by means of that place of honour and that power —if that achievement is right and helpful, that is, if it serves to promote the well-being of the common people, for as we have already argued, this well-being is according to God's intention. . . . So then, no one is debarred from devoting himself to the pursuit of truth, for that involves a praiseworthy kind of leisure. But high position, although without it a people cannot be ruled, is not in itself a respectable object of ambition, even if that position be held and exercised in a manner worthy of respect. We see then that it is love of truth that looks for sanctified leisure, while it is the compulsion of love that undertakes righteous engagement in affairs.

   * P. Brown, *Augustine of Hippo* (Berkeley: University of California Press, 1967).
 ** St. Augustine, *Concerning the City of God Against the Pagans*, translated by Henry Bettenson (Harmondsworth, England: Penguin, 1972), pp. 880–881.

Action and contemplation, doing and being, are not irreconcilable opposites but the two ends of a continuum. Even a hermit cannot live a life of exclusive contemplation, and the most hyperactive person stops and thinks once in a while. So the practical question is not which life-style to pursue, but what combination of the two modes should define your life.

Although one or another mode tends to predominate in a given life, the mix or balance between action and contemplation need not be fixed. Some periods call for and make possible more action than contemplation, others for more contemplation than action. In the Hindu concept of the male life cycle, youth is a time of apprenticeship. In young adulthood, one becomes a householder, but after the tasks of building a family and doing the work of the world are completed, a gradual separation from all ties of selfhood and community leads to a life of asceticism and total renunciation of the world.[18]

The dilemma we face in the modern world is that we keep getting stranded in one or the other realm: a life of contemplation with no power or opportunity for influencing events, or a life of action with little opportunity for reflection and inner growth. The ramifications of this dilemma pervade every aspect of our lives. We are either working and have too much to do and too little leisure, or we have retired and have too little to do and too much leisure. We either live cramped together in marriage, or feel incomplete in unmarried solitude. Like a pair of magnets we stand far apart or are stuck together.

It is not easy to break out of these patterns. But if there is a time when we can exercise a measure of control and autonomy in fashioning our lives while retaining our ties and discharging our responsibilities, fifty is as good a time as any.

When all is said and done, what matters most is not what you have wrought but how you have lived your life; not what you have done but who you have been. During the first fifty years of life, the blunders of youth and the exigencies of living may exonerate you for failing to be all that you could be or wanted to be. But at fifty it is time to attain the fullness of manhood and womanhood with that ineffable quality of maturity which combines knowledge with experience, judgment with wisdom, realism with hope, and skepticism with faith.

In a speech to the senior class at Princeton in 1954, Adlai Stevenson expressed the essence of being fifty:

What a man knows at fifty that he did not know at twenty is, for the most part, incommunicable. The laws, the aphorisms, the generalizations, the universal truths, the parables and the old saws—all of the observations about life which can be communicated handily in ready, verbal packages—are as well known to a man at twenty who has been attentive as to a man at fifty. He has been told them all, he has read them all, and he has probably repeated them all before he graduates from college; but he has not lived them all.

What he knows at fifty that he did not know at twenty boils down to something like this: The knowledge he has acquired with age is not the knowledge of formulas, or forms of words, but of people, places, notions—a knowledge not gained by words but by touch, sight, sound, victories, failures, sleeplessness, emotion, love—the human experiences and emotions on this earth and of oneself and of other men; and perhaps, too, a little faith, and a little reverence for things you cannot see.[19]

NOTES

Chapter 1

1. Stanley Brandes, *Forty: The Age and the Symbol* (Knoxville: University of Tennessee Press, 1985). Brandes advances the thesis that our use of age forty to designate a life phase is in part due to the symbolic meaning that number has carried since ancient times. A similar case could be made for fifty.
2. M. von Franz, *Time* (New York: Thames and Hudson, 1978).
3. Clifton Fadiman, "On Being Fifty," *Holiday*, vol. 17, no. 2 (February 1955).
4. Ezra Pound, "The River Merchant's Wife: A Letter." In *American Poetry and Prose*, Norman Foerster, ed. (Boston: Houghton Mifflin, 1957), p. 1340.
5. Carl Jung, *The Portable Jung*, edited by Joseph Campbell, translated by R.F.C. Hull (New York: Viking Press, 1971).
6. Ivan Turgenev, *Fathers and Sons*, translated by Constance Garnett (New York: Modern Library, 1950), Chapter 7.
7. Bernice L. Neugarten, "Adaptation and the Life Cycle," *Counseling Psychologist*, vol. 6, no.1 (1976): 16-20.
8. D.J. Levinson, C.D. Carrow, E.B. Klein, M.H. Levinson, and B. McKee, *The Seasons of a Man's Life* (New York: Alfred A. Knopf, 1978).
9. For Erik Erikson's formulations of psychosexual development, see *Childhood and Society*, 2nd ed. (New York: W.W. Norton, 1963), Chapter 2. His scheme of psychosocial development is stated briefly in Chapter 7 of the same work but is more fully elaborated in *Identity and the Life Cycle* (New York: W.W. Norton, 1959), Part II; in *Identity: Youth and Crisis* (New York, W.W. Norton, 1968), Chapter 3; and in *The Life Cycle Completed* (New York: W.W. Norton, 1982).
10. A good example is Gail Sheehy's national bestseller, *Passages* (New York: E.P. Dutton, 1974).

11. O.G. Brim, Jr., "Theories of the Male Mid-Life Crisis," *Counseling Psychologist*, vol.6, no.1 (1976).
12. These issues are explored at length in O.G. Brim and J. Kagan, eds., *Constancy and Change in Human Development* (Cambridge: Harvard University Press, 1980).
13. George E. Vaillant, *Adaptation to Life* (Boston: Little, Brown, 1977).
14. J.E. Birren and K.W. Schaie, eds., *The Handbook of the Psychology of Aging*, 2nd ed. (New York: Van Nostrand Reinhold, 1985). Provides extensive discussions of the theory and methods in the study of the psychology of aging, biological and social influences on behavior, psychological applications to the individual and to society. For less technical general sources on adulthood and midlife, see D.C. Kimmel, *Adulthood and Aging*, 2nd ed. (New York: John Wiley, 1980); L.E. Troll, *Early and Middle Adulthood*, 2nd ed. (Monterey, Calif.: Brooks/Cole, 1985).
15. Carol Gilligan, *In a Different Voice* (Cambridge: Harvard University Press, 1982).

Chapter 2

1. Theories of aging are discussed in James F. Fries and Lawrence M. Crapo, *Vitality and Aging* (San Francisco: W.H. Freeman, 1981).
2. *Daily Mail*, London, January 20, 1961.
3. S.K. Whitbourne, *The Aging Body* (New York: Springer-Verlag, 1985). Also see C.E. Finch and L. Hayflick, eds., *Handbook of the Biology of Aging*, 2nd ed. (New York: Van Nostrand Reinhold, 1985).
4. Jane Fonda, *Women Coming of Age* (New York: Simon and Schuster, 1984).
5. For further information on the effects of aging on skin and ways of dealing with them, see C.K. Jacobson and C. Ettlinger, *How to Be Wrinkle-Free: Look Younger Without Plastic Surgery* (New York: Putnam, 1986); A.W. Klein and J.H. Sternberg, *The Skin Book* (New York: Macmillan, 1981).
6. J. Brody, "Diets and Exercise, Not Gimmicks, for a Healthful Lifetime," *New York Times*, July 16, 1986, p. 13. For a concise review of popular diets and their shortcomings, see Marian Burros, "Playing the Diet Game, Where Chances of Winning Are Slim," in the same source.
7. There are a large number of books on how to keep fit. See, for instance, K. Cooper, *The Aerobics Program for Total Well-Being* (Toronto: Bantam, 1983); M. Shangold and G. Mirkin, *The Complete Sports Medicine Book for Women* (New York: Simon and Schuster, 1985); J. Fonda, *Jane Fonda's New Workout and Weight Loss Program* (New York: Simon and Schuster, 1986).
8. For further reading on the various aspects of the care and maintenance of the body at midlife, see C. Hallowell, *Growing Old, Staying Young* (New York: William Morrow, 1985); J. Fonda, *Women Coming of Age* (New York: Simon and Schuster, 1984); C. Pesmen, *How a Man Ages* (New York: Ballantine, 1984); D. Donohugh, *The Middle Years* (Philadelphia: Saunders, 1981).

Chapter 3

1. D. Symons, *The Evolution of Human Sexuality* (New York: Oxford University Press, 1979).
2. The *Guinness Book of World Records* credits Mrs. Vassiliyev, a Russian peasant, with 69 children born through 27 pregnancies (including four sets of quadruplets). The paternity record is held by Moulay Ismail ("the Bloodthirsty"), King of Morocco in the eighteenth century, who reportedly fathered 548 sons and 340 daughters.

3. For a general source on various aspects of human sexuality as well as for studies of the prevalence and frequency of sexual activity, see Herant Katchadourian, *Fundamentals of Human Sexuality*, 4th ed. (New York: Holt, Rinehart and Winston, 1985).

4. For a more detailed discussion of the hormonal basis of sexuality, see John Bancroft, *Human Sexuality and Its Problems* (Edinburgh: Churchill Livingstone, 1983).

5. These and related studies are discussed in Z. Luria and R.G. Meade, "Sexuality and the Middle-Aged Woman," in *Women in Midlife*, edited by G. Baruch and J. Brooks-Gunn (New York: Plenum Press, 1984).

6. A.C. Kinsey, W.B. Pomeroy, and C.E. Martin, *Sexual Behavior in the Human Male* (Philadelphia: Saunders, 1948).

7. W.H. Masters and V.E. Johnson, *Human Sexual Response* (Boston: Little, Brown, 1966).

8. R.C. Kolodny, W.H. Masters, and V.E. Johnson, *Textbook of Sexual Medicine* (Boston: Little, Brown, 1979).

9. H.S. Kaplan, "Sexual Relationships in Middle Age," *Physician and Patient*, October 1983, pp. 11-20.

10. Francine du Plessix Gray, "Manners of Deceit and the Case for Lying," *Esquire*, vol. 88, no. 6 (December 1977): 134.

Chapter 4

1. For technique for improving recall, see R. West, *Memory Fitness Over 40* (Gainsville, Fla.: Triad, 1985).

2. These and related studies are summarized in D.C. Kimmel, *Adulthood and Aging*, 2nd ed. (New York: John Wiley, 1980), and in L.E. Troll, *Early and Middle Adulthood*, 2nd ed. (Monterey, Calif.: Brooks/Cole Publishing Co., 1985).

3. Erik Erikson, *Childhood and Society* (New York: W.W. Norton, 1963); *Identity and the Life Cycle* (W. W. Norton, 1959); *Identity, Youth and Crisis* (W. W. Norton, 1968); *The Life Cycle Completed* (W. W. Norton: 1982).

4. E. Erikson, *Childhood and Society*, 2nd ed. (New York: W.W. Norton, 1963), p. 267.

5. B.L. Neugarten, ed., *Personality in Middle and Late Life* (New York: Atherton Press, 1964), pp. 198-199. Also see B.L. Neugarten, ed., *Middle Age and Aging* (Chicago: University of Chicago Press, 1968).

6. B.L. Neugarten and N. Datan, "The Subjective Experience of Middle Age," in L.D. Steinberg, ed., *The Life Cycle* (New York: Columbia University Press, 1981).

7. A. Shuken and B.L. Neugarten, "Personality and Social Interaction," in B.L. Neugarten, ed., *Personality in Middle and Late Life* (New York: Atherton Press, 1964), pp. 149-158.

8. B.L. Neugarten, ed., *Personality in Middle and Late Life* (New York: Atherton Press, 1964), p. 190.

9. Anne Morrow Lindbergh, *Gift from the Sea* (New York: Pantheon, 1955).

10. Marie Dressler, *My Own Story* (Boston: Little, Brown, 1934), Chapter 4.

11. G. Greer, "Letting Go," *Vogue*, vol. 176, no. 5 (May, 1986): 141-143.

12. B. Neugarten and N. Datan, "The Subjective Experience of Middle Age," in L. Steinberg, ed., *The Life Cycle* (New York: Columbia University Press, 1981), pp. 282-283.

13. M.W. Lear, "Is There a Male Menopause?" *New York Times Magazine*, January 28, 1973, p. 10.

14. O. G. Brim, Jr., "Theories of Male Mid-Life Crisis," *Counseling Psychologist*, vol. 6, no. 1 (1976): 2-9.

15. D.J. Levinson, C.D. Carrow, E.B. Klein, M.H. Levinson, and B. McKee, *The Seasons of a Man's Life* (New York: Alfred A. Knopf, 1978).
16. G.E. Vaillant, *Adaptation to Life* (Boston: Little, Brown, 1977).

Chapter 5

1. "Marital Status and Living Arrangements," U.S. Bureau of the Census, *Current Population Reports*, series P-20, no. 389 (Washington, D.C.: U.S. Government Printing Office, 1984).
2. The impact of these demographic and other social factors on midlife and older women is discussed in M.R. Block, J.L. Davidson, and J.D. Grambs, *Women Over Forty* (New York: Springer, 1981)
3. National Center for Health Statistics, *Vital Statistics of the United States, 1980* (Washington, D.C.: Public Health Service, U.S. Government Printing Office, 1984), vol. III, tables 1-7.
4. D. Tennov, *Love and Limerence* (New York: Stein and Day, 1979).
5. This and related studies are discussed in L.E. Troll, *Early and Middle Adulthood*, 2nd ed. (Monterey, Calif.: Brooks/Cole, 1985).
6. M. Heins, S. Smock, and M. Stein, "Productivity of Women Physicians," *Journal of the American Medical Association*, vol. 236, no. 17 (October 25, 1976): 1961-1964.
7. National Center for Health Statistics, *Vital Statistics of the United States, 1980* (Washington, D.C.: Public Health Service, U.S. Government Printing Office, 1984), vol. III, table 2.12.
8. P. Blumstein and P. Schwartz, *American Couples* (New York: William Morrow, 1985), p. 32.
9. L. Weitzman, *The Divorce Revolution* (New York: The Free Press, 1986).
10. R.H. Jacobs, "A Typology of Older American Women," *Social Policy*, vol. 7, no.3 (1976): 34-39.
11. L.B. Rubin, *Women of a Certain Age: The Midlife Search for Self* (New York: Harper & Row, 1979), p. 153.
12. C.M. Parkes, "Effects of Bereavement on Physical and Mental Health: A Study of the Medical Records of Widows," *British Medical Journal*, vol.2 (1964): 274-279.
13. J. Bernard, *The Future of Marriage* (New York: Bantam Books, 1973).
14. C.H. Deutsch, "Older Women Pool Male Resources," *New York Times*, Feb. 5, 1986.
15. B.L. Neugarten and K.K. Weinstein, "The Changing American Grandparent," in *Middle Age and Aging*, edited by B.L. Neugarten (Chicago: University of Chicago Press, 1968).
16. E.M. Brody, "Women in the Middle," and "Family Help to Older People," *The Gerontologist*, vol.21, no.5 (1981): 471-480.
17. V. R. Fuchs, *How We Live* (Cambridge: Harvard University Press, 1983).

Chapter 6

1. M.L. Kohn and C. Schooler, "The Reciprocal Effects of the Substantive Complexity of Work and Intellectual Flexibility," in *Aging from Birth to Death: Interdisciplinary Perspectives*, edited by M. Riley (Boulder, Colo.: Westview Press, 1979).
2. B.L. Neugarten, "The Awareness of Middle Age," in *Middle Age and Aging*, ed. B.L. Neugarten (Chicago: University of Chicago Press, 1967), p. 92.
3. D.H. Powell and R.F. Driscoll, "Middle-Class Professionals Face Unemployment,"*Society*, vol.10 (Jan-Feb. 1973). For the devastating effects of joblessness

among scientists and engineers in the 1970s, see P.G. Leventman, *Professionals Out of Work* (New York: The Free Press, 1981).

4. D. Sommers and A. Eck, "Occupational Mobility in the American Labor Force," *Monthly Labor Review* (Jan. 1977): 3-19.

5. S. Arbeiter (1979), cited in Troll, p. 182. Also see H.S. Parnes et al., *The Pre-retirement Years*, vol. 4 (Ohio State University: Center for Human Resource Research, 1974).

6. D.L. Krantz, *Radical Career Change* (New York: The Free Press, 1978).

7. *Statistical Abstract of the United States—1986*, 106th ed. (Washington, D.C.: U.S. Bureau of the Census, 1985), p. 392.

8. V.R. Fuchs, *How We Live* (Cambridge: Harvard University Press, 1983).

9. R.C. Atchley, "Selected Social and Psychological Differences Between Men and Women in Later Life," *Journal of Gerontology*, vol.31, no.2 (1976): 204-211.

10. S.A. Hewlett, "Feminism's Next Challenge: Support for Motherhood," *New York Times*, June 17, 1986, p. 27.

11. M.R. Block, J.L. Davidson, and J.D. Grambs, *Women over Forty*, (New York: Springer, 1981).

12. National Academy of Sciences report cited in the *New York Times*, Dec. 12, 1985, p. 12.

13. Fuchs, pp. 170-172

14. B.J. Stein, *Financial Passages* (New York: Doubleday, 1985). Also see D. R. Nichols, *Life Cycle Investing* (Homewood, Ill.: Dow Jones-Irwin, 1985), p. 24.

15. H. Lehman, *Age and Achievement* (Princeton, N.J.: Princeton University Press, 1953).

16. W. Dennis, "Creative Productivity Between the Ages of 20 and 80 Years," *Journal of Gerontology*, vol. 21, no. 1: 1-8.

17. R.N. Bellah, "To Kill and Survive or To Die and Become," in *Adulthood*, ed. E. Erikson (New York: W.W. Norton, 1978), pp. 61-80.

18. E.E. Erikson, *Gandhi's Truth* (New York: W.W. Norton, 1969).

19. Quoted in William Attwood, *Making It through Middle Age: Notes in Transit* (New York: Atheneum, 1982), p. 107.

ABOUT THE AUTHOR

Dr. Herant Katchadourian has had a distinguished career at Stanford as both teacher and administrator since 1966. He has served as Dean of Undergraduate Studies and Vice Provost for Undergraduate Education, was for three years a University Fellow, and had the distinction of being the first University Ombudsman when that post was created in 1970. Another first was his introduction, in 1968, of Human Biology 10, or Human Sexuality. Since then, Professor Katchadourian's widely admired wit and skill as a lecturer have attracted over 10,000 students to the course.

A Professor of Psychiatry and Behavioral Science, Dr. Katchadourian is also Professor of Education (by courtesy) and a member of the faculty of the Program in Human Biology. His own training and experience have embraced two cultures: An honors graduate of the Medical School of the American University of Beirut, he first came to the United States in 1958 as a resident in psychiatry at the University of Rochester. A year's work at the National Institute of Mental Health in Bethesda, Maryland was followed by a return to Lebanon, where, under a grant from the U.S. Public Health Service, he conducted studies in the epidemiology of psychiatric illness.

A gifted writer, Dr. Katchadourian is the author of *The Fundamentals of Human Sexuality.* Now in its fourth edition, it is a classic in its field and has been translated into French, Spanish, and Portuguese. He is also the author of *The Biology of Adolescence* and *Human Sexuality: Sense and Nonsense;* coauthor of *Careerism and Intellectualism Among College Students;* and editor of *Human Sexuality: A Comparative and Developmental Perspective.*

Dr. Katchadourian has been four times selected outstanding professor and Class Day speaker by Stanford seniors. He received the Richard W. Lyman Award of the Stanford Alumni Associaton in 1984.

Series Editor: Miriam Miller
Production Coordinator: Gayle Hemenway
Cover and Book Design: Bob Ciano
Graphs and Charts: Nigel Holmes
Illustrations: Kim Wilson Eversz
Calligraphy: Tim Girvin

CREDITS

PAGE

12   Figure 1-1 adapted from L. Hayflick, "Why Grow Old?," *The Stanford Magazine*, vol. 3, no. 1 (Spring/Summer 1975): 36.

14   Figure 1-2 adapted from J.F. Fries and L.M. Crapo, *Vitality and Aging* (San Francisco: W.H. Freeman, 1981).

31   Figure 2-1 adapted from B.L. Strehler, S.D. Evert, H.B. Glass, and N.W. Shock, eds., *The Biology of Aging: A Symposium* (Washington, D.C.: American Institute of Biological Sciences, 1960), p. 23. Reprinted with permission.

39   Data for Figure 2-2 from National Center for Health Statistics, Public Health Service, *Health: United States, 1984* (Washington, D.C.: U.S. Government Printing Office, 1984).

46   Figure 2-3 adapted from *Time*, August 19, 1985.

50   Figure 2-4 adapted from *Time*, March 17, 1986.

63   Figure 3-1 adapted from Masters and Johnson, *Human Sexual Response* (Boston: Little, Brown, 1966). Reprinted by permission.

64   Figure 3-2 adapted from Masters and Johnson.

66   Figure 3-3 adapted from Masters and Johnson.

67   Figure 3-4 adapted from Masters and Johnson.

87   Figure 4-1 adapted from D.C. Kimmel, *Adulthood and Aging* (New York: John Wiley and Sons, 1980), 2nd ed., p. 36. Based on David Wechsler, *Manual for the Adult Intelligence Scale* (New York: The Psychological Corporation, 1955). Copyright © 1955 by The Psychological Corporation.

88   Figure 4-2 adapted from L.E. Troll, *Early and Middle Adulthood*, 2nd ed. (Monterey, Calif.: Brooks/Cole Publishing Co., 1985), p. 69. Based on J.L. Horn, "Organization of Data on Life-Span Development of Human Abilities," in L.R. Goulet and P.B. Baltes, eds., *Life-Span Developmental Psychology: Research and Theory* (New York: Academic Press, 1970).

105   Data for Figure 5-1 from National Center for Health Statistics, *Vital Statistics of the United States, 1980* (Washington, D.C.: Public Health Service, U.S. Government Printing Office, 1984) vol. III, table 1.7.

116   Data for Figure 5-2 from National Center for Health Statistics.

136   Figure 6-1 adapted from *Work in America*, report of a special task force to the Secretary of Health, Education and Welfare (Cambridge, Mass.: MIT Press, 1973), p. 16.

144   Figure 6-2 adapted from V.R. Fuchs, *How We Live* (Cambridge, Mass.: Harvard University Press, 1983), p. 165. Based on Employment and Training Administration, *Employment and Training Report of the President, 1981*, table A-5.

148   Figure 6-3 adapted from Robert J. Gordon, *Macroeconomics* (Boston: Little, Brown, 1978), p. 379. Copyright © by Little, Brown and Company (Inc.). Used by permission.

150   Figure 6-4 adapted from J. Botwinick, *Cognitive Processes in Maturity and Old Age* (New York: Springer Publishing, 1967), copyright © 1967 by Springer Publishing Company, Inc. Based on Harvey C. Lehman, *Age and Achievement* (Princeton, N.J.: Princeton University Press, 1953).

151   Figure 6-5 adapted from J. Botwinick. Copyright © 1967 by Springer Publishing Company, Inc. Based on Wayne Dennis, "Creative Productivity Between the Ages of 20 and 80 Years," *Journal of Gerontology*, vol. 21, no. 1:1–8.

162   Photograph by Chuck Painter, Stanford News and Publications.

THE PORTABLE STANFORD

This is a volume in The Portable Stanford, a subscription book series published by the Stanford Alumni Association. Portable Stanford subscribers receive each new Portable Stanford volume on approval. Books may also be ordered from the following list.

Human Sexuality: Sense and Nonsense by Herant Katchadourian, M.D.
Some Must Watch While Some Must Sleep by William E. Dement, M.D.
Is Man Incomprehensible to Man? by Philip H. Rhinelander
Conceptual Blockbusting by James L. Adams
The Galactic Club: Intelligent Life in Outer Space by Ronald Bracewell
The Anxious Economy by Ezra Solomon
Murder and Madness by Donald T. Lunde, M.D.
Challengers to Capitalism: Marx, Lenin, and Mao by John G. Gurley
An Incomplete Guide to the Future by Willis W. Harman
America: The View from Europe by J. Martin Evans
The World That Could Be by Robert C. North
Law Without Lawyers: A Comparative View of Law in China and the United States by Victor H. Li
Tales of an Old Ocean by Tjeerd van Andel
Economic Policy Beyond the Headlines by George P. Shultz and Kenneth W. Dam
The American Way of Life Need Not Be Hazardous to Your Health by John W. Farquhar, M.D.
Worlds Into Words: Understanding Modern Poems by Diane Wood Middlebrook
The Politics of Contraception by Carl Djerassi
The Touch of Time: Myth, Memory, and the Self by Albert J. Guerard
Mirror and Mirage: Fiction by Nineteen edited by Albert J. Guerard
Insiders and Outliers: A Procession of Frenchmen by Gordon Wright
The Age of Television by Martin Esslin
Beyond the Turning Point: The U.S. Economy in the 1980s by Ezra Solomon
Cosmic Horizons: Understanding the Universe by Robert V. Wagoner and Donald W. Goldsmith
Challenges to Communism by John G. Gurley
The Musical Experience: Sound, Movement, and Arrival by Leonard G. Ratner
On Nineteen Eighty-Four edited by Peter Stansky
Terra Non Firma: Understanding and Preparing for Earthquakes by James M. Gere and Haresh C. Shah
Matters of Life and Death: Risks vs. Benefits of Medical Care by Eugene D. Robin, M.D.
Who Controls Our Schools? American Values in Conflict by Michael W. Kirst
Panic: Facing Fears, Phobias, and Anxiety by Stewart Agras, M.D.
Hormones: The Messengers of Life by Lawrence Crapo, M.D.
The Gorbachev Era edited by Alexander Dallin and Condoleezza Rice
Wide Awake at 3:00 A.M.: By Choice or By Chance? by Richard M. Coleman
Under the Gun: Nuclear Weapons and the Superpowers by Coit D. Blacker

To order additional copies of this book or to add your name to The Portable Stanford subscriber list, just return this postage-paid card.

☐ Please send me _____ copy(ies) of 50: MIDLIFE IN PERSPECTIVE at $9.95 each (California residents add .70 tax). Price includes shipping and handling.

Mr./Ms. _____

Address _____

City _____ State _____ Zip _____

☐ Please send _____ gift copy(ies) with gift card to:

Mr./Ms. _____

Address _____

City _____ State _____ Zip _____

☐ Payment enclosed.   ☐ Bill my Visa/MasterCard (circle one).

acct. # _____ exp. date _____

Price subject to change.

☐ Add my name to The Portable Stanford subscriber list. (Each new book will be sent on approval.)

☐ Please send me the following Portable Stanford volume(s): _____

_____

See back order card for prices (California residents add 7% tax). Price includes shipping and handling.

☐ Please send me _____ PS book bag(s) at $9.95 each (California residents add .70 tax). This includes shipping and handling.

Mr./Ms. _____

Address _____

City _____ State _____ Zip _____

☐ Payment enclosed.   ☐ Bill my Visa/MasterCard (circle one)

acct. # _____ exp. date _____

Price subject to change.

To order additional copies of this book or to add your name to The Portable Stanford subscriber list, just return this postage-paid card.

NO POSTAGE
NECESSARY
IF MAILED
IN THE
UNITED STATES

BUSINESS REPLY MAIL
FIRST CLASS   PERMIT NO. 67   PALO ALTO, CA

POSTAGE WILL BE PAID BY ADDRESSEE

The Portable Stanford
Stanford Alumni Association
Bowman Alumni House
Stanford, CA 94305

NO POSTAGE
NECESSARY
IF MAILED
IN THE
UNITED STATES

BUSINESS REPLY MAIL
FIRST CLASS   PERMIT NO. 67   PALO ALTO, CA

POSTAGE WILL BE PAID BY ADDRESSEE

The Portable Stanford
Stanford Alumni Association
Bowman Alumni House
Stanford, CA 94305